MW00439236

The ultimate source of h
ing legacy is an inspired
et fuel we need to prop
heights. Alise Cortez has drawn on her extensive experience and
research to write a comprehensive, insightful and highly readable
guide to living a life of meaning and purpose. I strongly recommend it!

Raj Sisodia, FW Olin Distinguished Professor of Global
Business, Babson College, andCo-founder &
Co-Chairman, Conscious Capitalism Inc.

To reach your highest purpose in life and work you could travel
the globe to talk to the world's greatest teachers and leaders and
dedicate many years to implementing their advice. Or you could
achieve a similar outcome far more quickly and with considerably
less expense by committing to this highly practical guide and applying the lessons that it makes available in a single integrated pathway
to transformation.

Paul Skinner, Author of Collaborative Advantage: How collaboration
beats competition as a strategy for success

Alise Cortez is the go-to guru for discovering one's purpose and
putting it into action. *Purpose Ignited* is equal parts inspiration and
information for those who are ready to put their purpose to work.

Sandra Duhé, Ph.D., MBA, Chair, Division of Corporate Communication
and Public Affairs, Southern Methodist University, Dallas, TX

We at DSM, in the private sector and the community need optimistic, self-aware, purpose led people now more than ever. The challenges we collectively confront cannot be met without them. This
potential lives within all of us and *Purpose Ignited* brings insight and
tools that enable this potential to be realized.

Hugh Welsh, President at DSM North America

Purpose Ignited offers very real, relevant and relatable content. So
many books talk about theory while Alise ensures you have insights,
information and inspiration that can be applied immediately.

Adrianne Court, Chief HR Officer, Alkami, and
Principal, Conscious Culture

Dr Alise Cortez has written a most insightful book that takes leaders and everyday workers on a most important journey to enliven our spirit, uncover our passion, find our meaning while elevating our self-care to live the most balanced life possible. Read this book slowly, digest the wisdom on every page and you will not regret the effort you made as the result is a most satisfying personal and professional life.

Arthur P. Ciaramicoli, Ed.D., Ph.D. Author of The Triumph of Diversity *and* The Soulful Leader.

Great leaders are driven, but what drives them goes beyond just self-interest. Values and larger purposes in life are just as important as economic incentives in motivating behavior, and in this insightful book Alise Cortez shows how "working on purpose" can unleash leadership potential. Taking her advice can make you a better leader—and a better person!

Ted Fischer, Professor of Anthropology

As a life-long lover of learning and meaningful connection, here I've found a treasure trove of tips and tools to playfully engage with life, make the most of every moment, and fully bring yourself to the sport of life and leadership.

Kimo Kippen, Aloha Learning Advisors, and former VP, Global Workforce Initiatives, and Chief Learning Officer at Hilton.

Inspired organizations not only perform, but excel towards their strategic goals. The insights Dr. Alise Cortez shares in *Purpose Ignited* are accessible tools to help you authentically lead from inspiration and purpose to unleash the potential of your organization and yourself!

Miranda McKinnon, Manager at Major Consumer Packaged Goods Company

If you want to be a great leader, you have a few options: you can either read through decades of research yourself, or personally track down great leaders and convince them to share their insights with you. Luckily for all of us, Dr. Cortez has already done both, and she presents her findings in a clear, easy-to-apply format. I recommend this book to anyone who wants to lead with purpose.

Dr. Michael Kannisto, MindemicLab

Excellent resource and inspirational guide on how to move from success to significance and find your true purpose and passion. Purpose and passion harnessed can change the world.

Charmaine Solomon, Founder and Chairman of the Board, My Possibilities

Purpose Ignited is a must read for leaders, both experienced and aspirational, that want to lead with purpose and desire to make a lasting positive impact in this world. Alise sets out in detail how to identify your purpose and then pursue it. She challenges readers to understand who they are and then provides a number of tools and stories to enable and inspire your own personal purpose journey. After reading *Purpose Ignited*, I am more inspired and equipped to live my own unique life in service to others.

Ron K. Barger, Serviam Investors

In *Purpose Ignited*, Alise Cortez creates fresh and encouraging perspectives for the reader by drawing upon the best that science and psychology have to offer. She shows you a wide array of practical tools that work and work quickly while drawing back the curtain to reveal *why* and *how* they've worked so well for others. I recommend this book to any thoughtful reader who wants to reach further by building upon a well-informed foundation.

Marilyn Montgomery, PhD, LMHC, BCC, Founder of Wellspring Development

Dr. Alise Cortez has written a "must read" insightful book that will enrich you in becoming a better leader and person! She provides thoughtful ideas, critical examples, and creates pathways for new thinking. This book is truly transformative and inspirational!

Cary A. Israel, J.D., Executive Advisory Board CampusWorks, Inc; Chair of Jewish Community Relations Council Springfield, Illinois; and District President Emeritus of Collin College

Purpose Ignited is a timely invitation to reflect on how much of our well being is tied to our work, and therefore our entire lives. The depth and originality of Dr. Cortez's reflections on finding passion and energy in the work we do, and her insights into how everyone can discover a sense of purpose makes this a genuinely motivating read - let it inspire you!

Linda Crompton, President and CEO, Leadership Women, Inc.

Be a "Moment Hunter"... from meaning to purpose! *Purpose Ignited* activates the heart, mind, and soul to help us look through a different lens to create more joy in our career and in life. This book is the fuel needed to drive in "the lane of fulfillment" on this amazing journey. It's intentional, it's purposeful, and it's inspiring! Highly recommended!"

Bruce W. Waller, Armstrong Relocation Executive; Author of Find Your Lane *and* Milemarkers*; and host of Life in the Leadership Lane podcast*

What the world needs now, more than ever, is for each one of us to be aligned with our unique meaning and purpose. If you know you're ready to play a bigger game and leave this world better than you found it, *Purpose Ignited* is the obvious next step! By masterfully weaving decades of experienced as a corporate consultant with the wisdom of countless conversations with world thought leaders as a radio show host, Alise Cortez reveals how to get back on track to what matters most!

Neha Sangwan, MD, author of TalkRx: Five Steps to Conversations to Create Connection, Health & Happiness

I cannot think of anyone more capable or able to inspire others. Dr. Cortez's engaging book is full of practical advice, researched best practices, and thoughtful and deeply meaningful messages to enhance and deepen both personal and professional purpose.

Paul Scott, M.A., Learning and Development Professional, Dallas, Texas

One doesn't have to look far in any direction or in any walk of life to see the absence of leadership in our world. This book challenges us to fill that void by pointing out that we each have the capacity to do that and shows us how to ignite those unique passions that drive us to fill that leadership vacuum regardless of the role we fill. This is a book that I will keep close by and will turn to time and again when I need to re-ignite those things that drive me to be the leader I was meant to be.

Mark Snyder, Retired Information Technology Executive and Investor

Serving the public as a police officer is a calling. That calling requires passion, purpose, and emotional intelligence to navigate the challenges facing police officers daily. This book keeps me grounded and inspired to serve others. I highly recommend this book to anyone wanting to take their own best versions of themselves to a higher level.

Danny Barton, Chief of Police, Coppell Police Department

Purpose Ignited

How Inspiring Leaders Unleash Passion and Elevate Cause

Alise Cortez, PhD

First published in Great Britain by Practical Inspiration Publishing, 2020

ISBN   978-1-78860-200-6 (print)
            978-1-78860-199-3 (epub)
            978-1-78860-198-6 (mobi)

Practical Inspiration
PUBLISHING

Other works by this author:
Passionately Striving in "Why": An Anthology of Women Who Persevere Mightily to Live Their Purpose, 2021

Contents

Acknowledgments

The first person I have to thank for this book is Roland Haertl for opening my eyes to a whole new world of possibility that I simply could never have imagined prior to our meeting. To my parents, Don and Sami Taylor, who passed away 28 days apart in January 2019, I thank you for teaching me early in life the beauty of work – that it is a way of life, and that in service of our work we are noble beings. Thanks too for always treating me as a capable, competent person – a gift that gave me confidence early in life and that has served me so well.

Michael Rochelle, I thank you from the bottom of my heart for appreciating my early research on modes of engagement and your ongoing encouragement and expectation to write about my work. (Although this is not *that* book, it *is* coming next!) My thanks to Shawn Anderson for always believing in me and coaching me to 'go the extra mile' for my dreams and live the life I so badly wanted for myself. You rescued me and have very much been the wind beneath my wings since we began working together in August 2017. To Henda Salmeron, thank you for your beautiful and inspiring friendship; you have always encouraged me to live life adventurously and go heartily after my goals and dreams – and you have been someone I wanted to emulate as an author and adventurer in life. Sherri Elliott-Yeary, thank you for your gift of friendship, example as speaker and author, and support. To Gabi Cortez, my daughter, you have my eternal gratitude for hanging in with me as I navigated my journey post-divorce these past few years and transformed into the person I wanted to become on the other side. It has been a rough ride for you, and I love you, precious wonder, more than you will ever know. Thanks to Amy Walters for finding me in the first place when you moved from the east coast to Dallas, and for gently but firmly goading me to get this book written.

This is the true joy in life – being used for a purpose recognized by yourself as a mighty one; being thoroughly worn out before you are thrown on the scrap heap; being a force of nature instead of a feverish selfish little clod of ailments and grievances complaining that the world will not devote itself to making you happy.

– George Bernard Shaw

Introduction

I wrote this book to turn you ON – to ignite you from the core of your being and radically alter your molecules! It is designed to help you discover much more deeply the unique gift you are in order to better the world through the contributions of your passion and purpose. The world is crying out for effective leaders who inspire people to realize their own greatness and elevate business to address the innumerable ails of the world. It starts with *you*. Your transformation into this inspirational leader igniting the impassioned contributions of everyone you touch awaits.

The contents are designed to vitally inspire you to cultivate meaning, passion, and purpose in the everyday moments, unleashing the very best version of you, every day. Then, *bring it* – and bring it *strong* to everything you do to make the contribution worthy of your one, precious life. And please ... bring that passionate, inspired person to work and insist that it informs your leadership, whether you are currently in such a capacity or working to get there. People are motivated at their highest levels when they can connect their work contributions to a greater purpose and mission. The world desperately needs a sea change in an otherwise soul-sucking workplace that is draining the life out of its members. I am asking *you* to be that force, standing tall in inspiration and purpose, that casts the vitalizing ripple through your team and through your organization. Work and the way business are done can be such profoundly powerful contributions that elevate humanity – your stewardship forward is what we need.

More specifically, this book is for two kinds of people. It is for existing leaders serious about their role in impacting the lives of their team and the direction of their company, and who always strive for ongoing growth, development, and improvement – never settling for 'good enough.' It is also for the man or woman aspiring to develop the capacity to live with passion, work with purpose, and step into leadership. Consider it your invitation to officially quit 'the walking dead' – a phrase I use to describe people who are unmindfully going through the motions in life – running the hamster wheel, dropping into bed at night exhausted, only to repeat the same experience the next day.

When you look back on your life, what mark will you have made on others' lives? What will be the value of the relationships you cultivated? Will you have made the world a better place? Will you be missed? How so? (Think about that one a little.) People want to know they *matter*, that their lives have meant something to others. I can't imagine the person who secretly hopes, 'Gee, I hope I can fly under the radar and no one will notice I've been here on the planet.' When people believe they matter, they are fulfilled and have a full tank to take good care of themselves and help others realize their talents and potential.

In my work as a management consultant developing leaders and organizations, I have witnessed people daily 'mailing it in,' giving only a portion of themselves and their talents and receiving little fulfilment, apart from the paycheck. When speaking to audiences, I often ask them what they're passionate about and am astounded at the quiet and confused response: 'I don't know.' So many people seem to be leading quiet lives of desperation; they are exhausted and have given up on ever having the relationships they want with their kids and significant others, feeling passionate about their lives or going for the next level in their career. The alarming increase in opioid addiction and suicide are testimony that society's ills need to be addressed urgently. I offer that learning to find meaning, passion, and purpose in life and work, in service to others, is key to avoiding these pitfalls, living your best life and realizing your potential.

Leaders in organizations are apathetic about their workforce and many have succumbed to the belief their employees only want a paycheck in exchange for as little output as they can get away with. Yet leaders and organizations have a tremendous capacity – and, I argue, responsibility – to profoundly and positively impact the wellbeing of the people whose lives they touch. That includes those in their workforce and the communities in which they live. Business in the capitalist system can be such a force for good; it just takes being mindful and conscientious about the cascading operational effects on all stakeholders – customers, employees, suppliers, investors, collaborating partners, community, and certainly the surrounding environment.

As a previous card-carrying member of the 'walking dead,' this book is my own roadmap out of apathy and resignation, to living with passion and working on purpose. I share what I have learned through this journey, which is heavily informed by an education grounded in positivist and existential psychology and logotherapy – Viktor Frankl's optimistic approach to life based on the belief that meaning is humankind's principal concern. You will become acquainted with key concepts from these foundational psychological elements through this book. If you wish to take a deeper dive, I highly encourage you to read Dr Martin Seligman's work on positivist psychology[1] and Dr Viktor Frankl's various works on existential psychology and logotherapy, starting with his seminal work *Man's Search for Meaning*.[2]

This book is also a reflection of the program I created called *Vitally Inspired – Living and Leading from Purpose*. That content is drawn from two decades working in management consulting and employee engagement, the meaning in work and identity research launched in my PhD program, and the

---

[1] M. Seligman, *Flourish: A Visionary New Understanding of Happiness and Wellbeing*, 2011.

[2] V. Frankl, *Man's Search for Meaning*, 1959.

Working on Purpose radio program I have hosted each week since February 2015, which affords me ongoing 'continuing education.' I source as guests specific subject matter experts and business leaders who I believe advance the conversation and practice of living with passion, working on purpose, and elevating cause in the way they do business. The work I've done over the last decade has convinced me that work is *not* working for a lot of people and that there is a better way forward.

This book is designed to equip you to live with passion, work with purpose, and lead with inspiration to take your team and business to completely new heights while generating healthy profits and having a positive societal impact. The first six chapters of this book (Part 1) contain the necessary components you will need to develop in yourself to become an inspirational leader working from purpose. Starting with *meaning* and finishing with *purpose*, each chapter builds on the previous one and offers exercises or poses questions that you can use as your laboratory to continually nurture and develop competency in that area.

In Chapter 1, we will distinguish meaning as an infinite source of motivation and enrichment to your life, help you recognize the extreme creative control you have over this precious resource, and take a tour of ways in which you can cultivate it to power your life. Chapter 2 takes a deep dive into identity and the importance of fully knowing *who you are* and *who you are striving to become*, and guides you through some practices to help you get much better acquainted with yourself to enable you to fully unleash your purpose. You will need to take extreme care of yourself along this journey, which is why key elements of wellbeing that help generate vitality are covered in Chapter 3.

Creating a fulfilling life and becoming an inspirational leader require giving deeply of yourself, unleashing your very best effort and creativity through the cultivation and expression of your passions, which is the focus of Chapter 4.

You will learn how to find avenues through which to resurrect and nurture lost and yet-to-be-discovered passions. Chapter 5 describes how your life will be exponentially expanded and enriched when you learn to be fully present to the myriad inspirations available to you – if only you can learn to 'look' and be open to their gift. That will involve letting down the protective guards that you've learned to use to steel yourself against guilt, shame, pain, and disappointment. You can make such a profound difference to the world when you live and work from purpose, in genuine service to others, as discussed in Chapter 6.

The last three chapters (Part 2) address work, your leadership, and the promise of doing business mindfully as a stakeholder capitalist within your organization. Chapter 7 focuses on the domain of work, as it is such a profoundly orientating or anchoring aspect of life. Work can span the spectrum of dismal drain to fantastic playground in which to realize your potential, and it is well worth the effort involved to optimize it for yourself and your team members. Chapter 8 covers purpose-inspired leadership and teaches you to cultivate it in a way that is uniquely authentic to yourself. You will become acquainted with the tremendous good that can be unleashed in the world when inspirational leaders working from purpose steward organizations that provide a meaningful experience that elicits passion and inspired performance while brightly coloring what according to purpose and leadership expert Zach Mercurio amounts to an estimated 40% of employees' lives.[3]

Finally, in Chapter 9 you will take a tour of the landscape of new and fresh ways in which business is being done to honor purpose and entice people to want to come to work and give their best. Work takes up at least a third of our lives, and according to the Gallup Organization (www.gallup.

---

[3] Mercurio, Z., *The invisible leader: Transform your life, work and organization with the power of authentic purpose*, 2017.

com), about 85% of the global workforce does not want to face it on Monday morning (or whenever their official work week begins). That's a travesty that I stand to correct, and I am asking you to join me in force. Life is just too precious to spend it slogging through a work day or work week.

This is your journey into passion, inspiration, and purpose – and I ask you to lean in, read closely and do the exercises, radio listening, and video viewing in order to facilitate the transformation that beckons you. To illustrate key concepts, I have added stories from my own life, consulting, and speaking, and from the *Working on Purpose* radio program. *Working on Purpose* is syndicated on more than 28 online platforms, though the dates I reference for the podcast correspond with those on the host page on VoiceAmerica.[4] I encourage you listen to those highlighted episodes that most resonate with you. Each chapter includes a set of exercises to help you apply or further think through the ideas, with templates to download and videos to watch that illustrate further how to apply the concepts. You'll find them at www. gusto-now.com and www.alisecortez.com. Get a new journal and use it as your guide to capture key takeaways and track your own transformation as you read through the book. Roll up your sleeves and let's get to *living and working from purpose!*

---

[4] www.voiceamerica.com/show/2429/working-on-purpose

Part 1

Getting You Fit for Life and Leadership

1

Meaning: Your Ultimate Source of Energy

It is virtually impossible not to encounter the word 'meaning' in the course of everyday life. It is everywhere and yet nowhere at the same time. But make no mistake about it – meaning is not far adrift from your survival needs of air, water, and food. Meaning is your ultimate motivator. When you think of the word 'meaning', what you're really referring to is that which is significant to you, matters to you, and resonates with your core essence. Meaning is how you make sense of the world and your place in it. Meaning is registered in the limbic brain alongside attention, emotions, and memory. Cultivating meaning in and across your life ought to exist on the same level as brushing your teeth, taking vitamins, sleeping, and exercising. Basic. Fundamental. Foundational.

People want meaningful work. They want meaningful relationships. And distinguishing what meaning actually is and how to access it in life and work is critically important to health and wellbeing – and, I would add, effectiveness – in today's world. This chapter will take you on an odyssey into the adventures of meaning that will give you access to painting colors across the canvas of your life and leadership in ways you never thought you could create.

Here you will become much more acquainted with the word 'meaning' in order to distinguish it for yourself and others you care about. First, you'll be introduced further to logotherapy and learn how to fold its optimistic approach to living into your own life. I'll ask you to seriously take stock of what you are doing with the precious existence you've been granted. We'll gaze from inside your brain at what calls your attention in the world, which becomes the lens through which you tend to look at most of life. And that exercise will help you lay the groundwork for discovering your general operational mindset so you can get access to upgrading it if useful, or building on it if it is already in a good state. Next, you'll get to see how adversity and the way you greet its entry into your life give you access to another level of meaning that distinguishes you and offers the opportunity to elevate yourself above everyday life. Cultivating and expressing gratitude is your last stop in this chapter; it is a practice that, when done well, will likely lower your blood pressure while increasing your serotonin levels in the brain. Roll up your sleeves, get to work, and enjoy the journey.

Logotherapy as a Way of Life

You were briefly acquainted with Dr Viktor Frankl and logotherapy in the introduction of this book, and here you will take a deeper dive to start your journey into the transformation this book intends for you. Dr Frankl was a physician specializing in neurology and psychology. He initially worked in the late 1920s to help address the alarming teen suicide rate in Vienna. He developed his meaning-centered approach toward psychological wellbeing before surviving three years in the Nazi concentration camps during World War II and actually entered the camps with his precious manuscript, describing it as his only important possession (which was later destroyed by the guards and recreated during his incarceration). He considered his personal experience an affirmation of the theory he conceived about meaning serving as the central driver of human motivation. He witnessed countless fellow victims of the Holocaust lose their ability to conjure meaning, then their will to live, and soon succumb to death.

Frankl lost his wife and parents in the Holocaust and emerged as a philosopher further convicted of his own work. In fact, he earned a PhD in 1948 as he further investigated and solidified his theory on existential psychology, a testament to his dedication to the field, having already earned an MD in 1930.

I initially became acquainted with logotherapy in the late 1990s, when I began my PhD program, as I delved deeply into the psychology and sociology that informed my human development studies. Over the past decade or so, Frankl's work has taken on a more central prominence in both my own life and the consulting and speaking I do. I can't help but consistently notice clients and speaking audiences articulating that they want something *more*, but don't know what it is. I've come to understand that they are articulating the absence of meaning. They want more from life. They want to matter. Logotherapy is a way to access all those things, which is why I personally practice it and fold its tenets into my programs, consulting, and speaking.

The word 'logotherapy' is based on *logos* (meaning) and therapy (the application of), and as a philosophy and application of psychology holds three core assumptions:

1. Life has meaning under all circumstances, even the most miserable ones.
2. Our main motivation for living is our will to find meaning in life.

3. We have freedom to find meaning in what we do and what we experience, or at least in the stand we take when faced with a situation of unchangeable suffering.[1]

My attraction to logotherapy is due to its optimism, focus on wellbeing, and the central tenet that meaning is the prime motivation in life. Life is not a quest for pleasure or power, but rather a quest for meaning. Logotherapy teaches that there are no tragic or negative aspects that cannot be transmuted into positive accomplishments by the attitudinal approach one takes to them. Logotherapy and the Franklian psychology that informs it hold there are three principal ways of finding meaning – both in the moment and as ultimate meaning:

1. *Creative* – what you give to the world in terms of creations
2. *Experiential* – what you take from the world in the way of encounters and experiences
3. *Attitudinal* – the stand you take to all predicaments when you face a fate you cannot change.

I have come to associate these ways of meaning with specific terms that speak to my messaging, as follows:

1. *Creative:* what we give to the world in terms of creations = PASSION.
2. *Experiential:* what we take from the world in the way of encounters and experiences = INSPIRATION.
3. *Attitudinal:* the stand we take to all predicaments when we face a fate we cannot change, whatever it might be = MINDSET.

---

[1] Frankl, *Man's Search for Meaning.*

A crisis of meaning is occurring on a global scale, which is draining the life out of people and the organizations that employ them. People hunger for meaningful connection with others, work that is purposeful and to enjoy a bigger, more beautiful life. The absence of meaning shows up in the escalating rates of opioid use and suicide as people seek to numb the vacuousness of their lives. In that space of emptiness, people seek *something* more without knowing why and often end up getting divorced or changing jobs, unknowingly looking for meaning.

Yet, on the work front where you spend such a significant portion of your life, there is so much that you, other leaders and organizations can do to shift this tide of meaninglessness and humanize the workplace. A number of meaning (and purpose) crusaders have set out to change the way work is experienced. One of the most prominent I've encountered is Dr Alex Pattakos, aka 'Dr Meaning'.[2] Alongside his wife and business partner Elaine Dundon, he works with business and governmental organizations to help members access life-giving meaning to their work. This is done through their discipline called 'MEANINGology', which is designed to advance the human quest for meaning in life, work, and society. My own approach starts with this book and the Vitally Inspired – Living and Leading Through Purpose programs and consulting I have created.

Your invitation awaits. By incorporating logotherapy into your life and your practice of leadership, you can gain infinite access to the deep well of meaning that will fill your tank with high-octane fuel. Once you accept that meaning is everywhere and your opportunity is to discover it for the rest of your life, you will charter an irreversible path and enroll eager followers along the way whose lives and journeys will be enriched by your touch. This is where you open your fresh journal and start to record your thoughts and responses to what you are

---

[2] *Working on Purpose* episode 231, Voice America, 7/10/2019.

reading. You are officially on the path to take on life in a more meaningful way than before you encountered this book.

What Will You Do with Your One, Precious Life?

Let's now turn this conversation into a much more personal one. I often challenge my speaking audiences with this question, and I'll do the same for you: What will you do with your *one, precious life?* I believe this famous question is often attributed to Marianne Williamson and has certainly been uttered by countless other notables. Simple and yet direct, the inquiry forces a certain sobriety. At its heart, this question concerns what you will make your life *mean* and how it will *count.* Getting serious and intentional about what your life looks like is critical. No more sleep-walking through life, okay? How many days – or *summers,* as my South African friend Henda Salmeron says – do you have, and what will you do with them?[3]

Unavoidably, living with an unknown expiration date comes with existence. We all know we have a finite amount of time on the planet but don't know the length of our stay. This can produce a great urgency *when you become attuned to it.* I beg *you* to take up that torch for yourself; the rest of the book will give you an approach to just how to do so. In your acceptance of this finite nature of life, you will come to see it as good for your health, fulfillment, and wellbeing, and also how everyone you encounter across your life benefits.

Another, perhaps more sobering, question is how you will answer for the one life you have been given. Have you ever considered just how incredible it is that *you* exist? I'm asking you to consider this question *before* life prompts you with a

---

[3] Henda Salmeron's website, https://hendasalmeron.com.

severe inquiry or incident – like a major illness or catastrophic event. I've met a number of people through my *Working on Purpose* radio show who have begun living radically only after life whacked them hard with major adversity. One such person who has indelibly left a reminder on me about fully living our one, precious life is Gwen Rich.[4] Gwen is a wife and mother of four, an accredited image-stylist, small business owner, philanthropist, and author of *Stop Complaining – Make Your Own Luck*. After eight years and eight misdiagnoses, Gwen was ultimately diagnosed with incurable metastatic breast cancer in 2012. It isn't a question of if, but rather when for her.

Gwen has managed to live several years beyond her 'expiration date,' as she calls it. Struggling to decide what to do with the time she had left, she launched The Gwen Marie Collection *Purses with a Purpose* in 2014. This quality luxury handbag collection is 100% made in America and portions of the proceeds are donated to the University of Chicago Medicine for cancer research. Her *Legacy-on-the-Go* is the development of an online teaching community called The Rich Solution. It is a place where people in her known community and the extended community she is building can come and learn from her journey. The Rich Solution online community will also help to raise money for cancer research as well as fuel the passions of others who dare to turn their worst nightmares into their most meaningful life experiences.

Before her diagnosis, Gwen told me she struggled with her purpose. She had a great life, but something was missing. It took some events and getting cancer for her to find her purpose and begin feeling truly fulfilled by her life. Gwen took a stand when she received her diagnosis and did not feel sorry for herself. Her passion gave her the energy to feel good about getting up every day. The legacy she is working to leave behind is to inspire people to take action and not

---

[4] *Working on Purpose* episode 186, Voice America, 8/29/2018.

have to go through trauma or cancer like she has. Gwen is a reminder to avoid filling life with material things and instead find your passion, because experiencing those strong emotions really fuels purpose. For me, Gwen will always be my reminder to be mindful of just what it is I'm doing with my own one, precious life.

Your Lens: Your Unique Vantage Point

At its simplest, meaning can be thought of as the unique lens through which you see the world, interpret it, and make sense of it. Think of your lens as your very own kaleidoscope that filters and fashions your every observation and interaction with the world. Only *you* can see the world as you do. You are the ultimate prescribing doctor that determines the lens you use to experience life and make meaning of the innumerable events and interactions that happen in your precious existence. It is *your* choice, your declaration and, upon close examination, an expression of your unique being in the world. Your lens is also incredibly malleable, a reflection of the limitless potential bestowed on you as a human being, and it will change focus as you continue to unfold and transform yourself over time.

What's your personal lens prescription? My lens sees the world as a beautiful place that nonetheless needs my energy, passion, and the exercise of my purpose to keep it moving on an upward, growing trajectory. Your opportunity is to identify your specific lens on the world that is uniquely you – and very likely, an expression of your purpose. Becoming aware of your unique lens helps you understand why some things matter much more than others, why you probably do the work you do, and why you are connected with the particular significant other you are. Your lens dictates what you pay attention to and give yourself over to. Your lens makes it *obvious* to you what you pour yourself into, although when you gain a deeper understanding of why that particular focal point matters to you, you are able to distinguish your contribution and can seek ongoing ways to further refine your perspective.

What if you could distinguish your work lens the way Dr Mary Howard does?[5] She sees the world through a lens something like this: Everything is about education and work is a way of life. Dr Howard does her work with complete passion and joy, thoroughly reveling in her efforts with educators to help them increase their impact in the classroom. She loves helping them recapture the passion for their work that they may have lost at some point along the way. Dr Howard has spent more than four decades in her education career and sees an opportunity to constantly improve education and increase the joy connected with it.

At the time of our conversation in mid-2016, Dr Howard proclaimed that she had no plan to retire. Why would she, when she's having so much fun?! When I asked Dr Howard why she was so passionate about her work, she replied thoughtfully:

> *I get to spend the bulk of my time – and I'm choosing that word on purpose – with educators who make a difference in the lives of children; I get to spend time with children who give our work wings and heart; and I get to do the work that still makes me excited to get out of bed every morning. I get to do what makes my heart sing every day.*

She went on to say that she does not wait for passion to tap her on the shoulder, but rather works 'daily to *feed* her passion and hold on to it for dear life'. Hang on to that bit about passion – it will be covered in depth in Chapter 4. Meanwhile, let's take a step back to see the bigger picture framed by your lens and talk about your mindset.

---

[5] *Working on Purpose* episode 66, Voice America, 5/4/2016.

Mindset: Your Governing Star

Mindset is a collection of attitudes informed by the lens you use to interpret the world and your experience in it. It can be thought of as an operating system and an overarching network connecting many prescriptive filters. Thus, if your filters include looking for details and data, looking for what's missing in an argument, and listening for how succinctly someone narrates a story, your mindset could be described as evaluative or analytical. Someone who sees meeting new people as play, looks for synergies between disparate people or companies, and takes delight in bringing people together to see what unfolds may be working from a possibilities mindset.

The underlying assumptions you have about yourself and the world are powerful governing forces. Yet the vast number of people do not understand – or are not aware or conscious of – the mindset that governs their way of thinking, feeling, and behaving. That mindset must be brought to the surface level of consciousness in order to enjoy the fullest expression of life and alter results where they may be lacking. Only by becoming conscious and aware of the mindset that governs you can you begin to intervene and create new ways of seeing the world and your place in it. Everyone makes all manner of assumptions about what is possible for them physically, professionally, socially, and mentally across life. The opportunity exists to become more frequently and fully attuned to the mindset that governs you.

You will learn more about why understanding your mindset is important in Chapter 3 when you learn about self-efficacy beliefs. By way of illustration, if you assume or believe you can't possibly run a marathon, you likely won't put in the effort to train, so your assumption will be confirmed. Believing you 'are' at whatever career level you're currently stationed at is a limiting belief that dramatically determines how far your career can progress.

Think of how you approach your everyday life. Which of these statements do you tend to employ?

- This is overwhelming! OR I got this!
- I failed. OR I learned what did not work.
- I can't. OR I'll find a way.
- I don't have any current/useful skills. OR I can learn what I set my mind to.
- I'm not worthy of this relationship. OR I have much to offer someone.
- I can only ask for X (minimum) salary. OR I'm worth Y (larger) salary and I need to ask for what I want and what I'm worth.

Over the years, I have coached men and women who are completely unaware of the aspects of their mindset that serve them well and those that are very limiting or destructive. Perhaps the most common limiting mindset is 'I can't.' I can't reach that leadership level. I can't go to college. I can't take a job that requires travel. I can't speak in public – I'm no good at it. The list of these limiting beliefs – which usually snuck into your consciousness at a previous, now inapplicable time – goes on and on. Where did they come from and how do you get rid of them or replace them with something else that will contribute better results?

How can you gain conscious access to your mindset? It helps to talk to others about what you believe about the world. Have them question where those beliefs come from and how those beliefs are serving you. You will probably be very surprised that many of the beliefs you hold as completely factual actually arose from a tender period in your childhood, as you formed a response from a stressful experience. In short, having conversations about your mindset with others helps you to hold up a mirror of yourself to yourself. An experienced coach can help tremendously, and so can friends, family, and colleagues. The key is to dialogue in curious interaction with your conversational partner in search for understanding, without defensively clinging to the past, history, or way of being that is manifested in your mindset.

Your leadership journey will provide you with a constant stream of opportunities to develop a healthy growth mindset, just as it did for Donald Thompson.[6] Referring to himself as 'the unlikely CEO,' because 'if one looks at my picture, if one looks at my pedigree, if one looks at my background, it doesn't seem likely some of the successes that I've had,' Donald credits much of his success in life to the way he sees the world and approaches its opportunities. He says:

> *In my mind, every single day that the sun comes up gives me the opportunity to be better, to do better, and to serve. And that mindset, in a very, very sincere way, means that I'm more passionate, I'm more committed, than most of the people that I'm competing with. So the motivation to do well was because I didn't want to squander any opportunity ... and I didn't believe someone else was responsible for my success. I believed that, as long as I had a reasonable opportunity – not even a fair opportunity, but a reasonable opportunity – to make it, it was up to me to turn that motivation into meaningful monetary gain for me and my family.*[7]

Donald went to college but did not finish his degree. He had his heart set on a career in the National Football League (NFL), but the world apparently had other plans for him. As he set out in his early days to navigate his career, prospective employers asked him, 'Why should I hire you when you didn't even finish college?' His response is indictive of the power of mindset: 'I'm gonna sell a million-dollars of software next year for someone. Either it will be you or your competitor. You choose. And, my college degree will have very little to do with whether that money comes into your company or someone else's.' He invariably got the job. He has since gone on to found a number of companies, author a book, and own a soccer team in India. And he does so with a spirit of reaching out to people he encounters to encourage the upward trajectory of their lives and careers.

Hugging Your Adversity to Stake a Claim to Yourself

Building on mindset, your attitude toward adversity and what you face in life is nothing short of – well, *everything*. From a logotherapeutic perspective, the way you make sense of inescapable hardship and difficulty is one of the three principal ways you create meaning in life. The other two are your creations, or what you give of yourself to the world (your passion), and your experiences and encounters, or what the world gives you (your inspirations). The meaning *you* give to adversity in your life is uniquely of your own creation – it does not just exist as a fact. No, your mindset and the way you make sense of difficult, harrowing or flat-out 'who does this stuff *happen to* in life?' events are completely of your own creation and under your control, and can absolutely be modified to improve mental wellbeing and functioning. Framed through an opportunistic growth lens, there's even better news: adversity helps us become the people we're *meant* to become, a perspective I completely share with radio guest Steve Gavatorta,[8] who wrote *In Defense of Adversity: Turning Your Greatest Challenges into Your Greatest Success.*[9]

---

[8] *Working on Purpose* episode 178, Voice America, 7/3/2018.

[9] S. Gavatorta, *In Defense of Adversity: Turning Your Greatest Challenges into Your Greatest Successes,* 2017.

Adversity comes in many shapes and sizes, and can come in the form of emotional, physical, professional, personal, social, financial, or spiritual challenges. Recall Viktor Frankl's words that the one thing you always have available is your choice of the attitude you take when confronted with a fate you cannot change. No one can ever take that choice away from you – although you can momentarily convince yourself that you do not have such an option. Never doubt the magnificence of the human spirit to persevere – it is truly breathtaking. Here's another perspective on adversity and the way you navigate through it: When you confront adversity and take it on as a worthy adversary, you will likely feel a sense of pride in yourself as you rise to the occasion. Furthermore, others who witness your handling of adversity will be inspired and emboldened by it, which only serves to catalyze their own courageous approach to challenges.

I have had the privilege of meeting countless people whose stories of overcoming adversity inspire me. It is likely that you have too, and I ask that you let that inspiration wash over you and be the wind beneath your wings as you navigate through your own challenges. If Staff Sergeant (Ret.) Jason Morgan's story, which I learned on air, does not illustrate the magnificence of the human spirit and the ability to use adversity to lean into and become who one is meant to be, I don't know whose does.[10] His story is a walking billboard for the efficacy of adversity in life and the unique way it is construed as meaningful.

Having enlisted in the US Air Force at the age of 22, Staff Sergeant Morgan served as a member of an elite unit that provided meteorological and combat support for special operations missions for almost ten years. In 1999, at age 29 and with just a few days left in his deployment in Ecuador with the 160th Special Operations Aviation Regiment on an undercover mission, Staff Sergeant Morgan came under fire by a militant terrorist group and suffered a broken back that left him paralyzed and in

---

[10] *Working on Purpose* episode 126, Voice America, 6/28/2017.

a coma for two months. That's just the beginning of his story, which is replete with one setback and adversity after another. He spent several years after his injury in the hospital in dozens of surgeries and treatments, often in debilitating pain, experiencing infections and later a leg amputation. Soon after leaving the Air Force, Staff Sergeant Morgan became a single parent when he and his wife divorced.

At the time of writing, Staff Sergeant Morgan has been in a wheelchair for 21 years. He has raised his three boys as a single dad, started a foundation to help others, and says giving back to others is the greatest thing he's ever done. He is a speaker and the author of *A Dog Called Hope: The Special Forces Wounded Warrior and the Dog Who Dared to Love Him.*[11] He told me he has many days when he feels significant pain and goes days without sleeping. But he also knows that there are men and women so much worse off than him. He chooses to focus on others, which takes the attention off himself. Staff Sergeant Morgan has chosen to impose a certain meaning on adversity, and he taught me that the best way to handle it is to start by expecting it. That way, when it does happen it's not so debilitating, and you'll be less likely to get down about it but will instead look for ways to improve the situation.

A couple of months after the episode aired, I invited Staff Sergeant Morgan to lunch, as we both live in the Dallas area. He had told me on air that one of the perks of being paralyzed in a wheelchair with a guide dog was that it put him in the enviable position of attracting women. At the restaurant, as he predicted, we were approached by numerous people – admittedly mostly women – who offered a treat or water for the dog and generally fawned over him. With an irrepressible wink and incorrigible flirtatiousness, Staff Sergeant Morgan turned to me and said, 'See what I mean?'

---

[11] J. Morgan and D. Lewis, *A Dog Called Hope: The Special Forces Wounded Warrior and the Dog Who Dared to Love Him,* 2017.

Could you handle this kind of ongoing adversity the way Staff Sergeant Morgan did? I hope you never have to, although you can be certain you will encounter your own set of adversities in life and along your leadership journey. Standing in Staff Sergeant Morgan's example, when those adversities do come calling, remember them for the gift they are, and see them as an opportunity to become who you're meant to be through your response. Definitely try to keep your sense of humor along the way.

On the Hunt for Gratitude: Be a 'Moment Hunter'

Gratitude is generated from the meaning you give to experiences and interactions. It's also a core ingredient of wellbeing, living with passion, and being an inspirational leader that people yearn to follow. By gratitude, I mean both the state of *being* grateful as well as the *act* of expressing gratitude. Learning to incorporate continuous gratitude in your life also contributes to better physical health, as people tend to report fewer aches and pains and instead focus on exercise. Psychologically, experiencing gratitude reduces the presence of toxic emotions like anger, frustration, and resentment, and is positively linked with happiness and reduced depression. Gratitude also helps to cultivate empathy while reducing aggression. Consider that empathy is also linked to increased self-esteem, in part because living with empathy reduces the tendency to make social comparisons. When you live with gratitude, you can appreciate the accomplishments of others without feeling inferior to them. Finally, cultivating gratitude is linked with increased mental strength and resilience. We learned from Staff Sergeant Morgan – who repeatedly said others had it worse than he did and expressed how grateful he was for having the chance to be of service to veterans and others who needed a dose of inspiration.

Cultivating a sense of gratitude – being more grateful – is an easy practice to add to your life, generating greater meaning. It can be as simple as vowing to observe one special moment or interaction a day and just appreciate it, letting that goodness wash over you. I heartily recommend incorporating the Japanese concept of *ichigo ichie* into your everyday life, as Hector Garcia taught me on air and in reading his book *The Book of Ichigo Ichie: The Art of Making the Most of Every Moment, the Japanese Way.*[12] *Ichigo ichie* can be translated as 'in this moment, an opportunity', which means roughly 'what we are experiencing right now will never happen again so we must treat it like a special treasure.' The call, then, is to participate wholeheartedly in every moment and become a 'moment hunter.'

One way to add another level of intentionality of gratitude and thus enjoy its accompanying psychological benefits is simply to keep a journal that captures three things for which you're grateful each day. This kind of reflection can be a nice way to send yourself off to sleep. In fact, gratitude is linked to good sleep. You can also make it a practice to ruminate on things for which you continue to be grateful. As an example, I will be forever grateful to my boss Roland Haertl who fired me at age 19. Although it was a shocking, sad, and uprooting experience at the time, Roland saw something much bigger in me than I could see for myself. Getting fired forced me out into the bigger world to pursue my formal education, travel, and professional evolution. He opened the door of possibility so wide and set me on a path toward self-development, ever seeking my own potential – which eventually helped me to identify that as a calling to help others do the same.

---

[12] *Working on Purpose* episode 270, Voice America, 4/8/2020.

That brings us to the expression of gratitude. I often tell Roland how much I appreciate him for what he has done for me in my life. For most of the past 17 years, I've visited him in person as I've passed through Portland, Oregon to see my family in the eastern side of the state, and we correspond through email and phone calls in between visits. Similarly, when my maternal grandmother was alive, I used to write her love letters addressed on the envelope to 'The Greatest Grandma on the Planet,' followed by her actual delivery address, and detail in the enclosed letter how much her kind and generous actions and my many memories of her had so beautifully contributed to my life. When we spoke on the phone, she would remark about the letters and their content with, 'You sure know how to make a little 'ole lady feel special.' I'd always reply, 'Good, 'cause that's how you always made me feel.' When practiced and expressed, gratitude makes everyone a little bigger. Learning to incorporate an ongoing expression of gratitude for your team's contributions is an essential practice as an inspirational leader. People *ache* to know they matter, and when you tell them how much they do, you elevate them and create a powerful contribution to their meaning tank.

Ikigai: A Framework for a Meaningful Life

In a world where so many people are desperately seeking greater meaning and a path to their purpose, the Japanese concept of *ikigai* (pronounced 'eek-e-guy') just might be the holy grail. *Ikigai* can be thought of as a framework for understanding who you really are while providing a way to live a more meaningful life. *Ikigai* is an interesting Japanese concept used to describe one's reason for the source of value in one's life, beyond anything financial. *Ikigai* is, above all else, a lifestyle that strives to balance the spiritual with the practical.

Ikigai comprises four aspects, and to pursue one's *ikigai* is to look for where these four aspects overlap. They are: what you love (your passion); what you are good at (your vocation); what you can get paid for (your profession); and what the world needs (your mission). This balance is found at the intersection where your passions and talents converge with the things that the world needs and is willing to pay for.

Justyn Barnes'[13] book, *Ikigai: Discovering Your Reason for Being*[14] is a well-organized, easy read with beautiful illustrations that complement the concepts described. I asked Justyn why he thought *ikigai* was such an important concept today. He echoed my thoughts that there seems to be an increasing move toward secular answers in the search for a meaningful life. He went on to say that with life today intermingled with automation, artificial intelligence, and robotics, humans are increasingly looking for where they fit in. He also reminded me that in today's fast-paced world, people struggle to find a work–life harmony and *ikigai* offers a way to harmonize our lives across the four important spheres or aspects of our lives: our passion, profession, vocation, and mission.

Justyn and I talked about the benefits of pursuing our *ikigai*. It was delightful to hear him, a British man, compare the American Declaration of Independence that deems the pursuit of happiness an inalienable right, with the Japanese context, where *ikigai* is a more highly valued aspiration. In Japan, *ikigai* offers a more nuanced, realistic view of wellbeing that invites us to find meaning and fulfillment not just in the occasional highs of life, but the lows and the humdrum of each moment too, allowing us to see each day as alive with meaning. Pursuing your *ikigai* gives you the space and practice to be present to all these glorious moments that make up your day and let the meaning you derive from them wash over you. *Ikigai* offers a framework to thread critical aspects

---

[13] *Working on Purpose* episode 241, Voice America, 9/18/2019.

[14] J. Barnes, *Ikigai: Discover Your Reason for Being*, 2018.

of your life and fold them all together neatly into one unified way to pursue your life meaningfully and with purpose.

Final Thoughts on Meaning

As a human being, you are a master of meaning-making. Your ability to make meaning from what you invest of yourself and encounter in the course of your life has been key to your survival. Becoming present to the reality that you really have just one, precious life helps ground you in the moment while enabling you to strive for a future of fulfilment and flourishing. The opportunity you have for your own growth and ongoing evolution is to become very attuned to your filters to the world and how you make sense of it – that is, to become attuned to your mindset. Becoming present to the mindset that governs you and intervening to transform it to one that enables you to exercise more human agency is a priceless opportunity. The way you allow yourself to see the world contributes heavily to your happiness, success, and the quality of your relationships.

You can count on challenges and problems as you navigate your life. It is your response to this adversity, what you learn from it, and how you grow that makes all the difference. As you do, summoning gratitude not only gives more meaning to the moment but is also an incredibly effective way to elicit wellbeing and peace. Practicing these activities in a way that cultivates meaning across your life represents an optimistic way of journeying through life, which is the essence of embracing logotherapy as a way of life, as Dr Pattakos, aka 'Dr Meaning,' reminds us.

As an incessant meaning-maker, you literally have total editorial control over the meaning you assign each and every interaction, every day, every hour, every moment. While that may sound daunting, I hope you will see it as quite liberating and empowering, and as a place from which to create the life you most desire. The power you have to ascribe meaning to your life, to play with it, hold it dear, and grow from it, is bottomless. One significant way to discover and cultivate meaning comes through what you give of yourself to the world – that is, your passions, the topic of Chapter 4. To situate yourself and get you thinking holistically, sketching the components of your *ikigai* is a way to start to frame meaning as considered from a Venn diagram, where passion, vocation, profession, and mission intersect. But first, let's get much better acquainted with you.

Key Points and Exercises

Logotherapy as a Way of Life
In your journal, brainstorm at least three ways in which you can start to fold a logotherapeutic approach and perspective to your life. Do the same with your leadership practice – how can adding a logotherapeutic perspective enrich your followers by giving them greater access to meaning?

What Will You Do with Your One, Precious Life?
Ask yourself these questions and write down your thoughts.

1) What would you do with your life if you knew you had a sooner-rather-than-later expiration date? 2) What if, say, you were told you have three months to live? 3) How would facing that finality alter the direction of your life? 4) Would it at all? 5) Wouldn't it be amazing if you lived in Gwen's example and worked on purpose to leave a legacy, even without a terminal diagnosis prompting the urgency?

Your Lens
What is the unique way you see the world – what is your lens on it? How is it distinguished from that of others? What do people exclaim about your perspective on things ('Wow, I never thought of that way!' Or, 'Hmm, you seem to take a very strategic approach to solving problems')? Look for what this lens indicates about the way you make meaning across your life and the way you see yourself.

Mindset
Download the Mapping Your Mindset template from www.alisecortez.com or www.gusto-now.com and use it to derive your values and attitude. Think about how they inform your mindset. In your journal, consider how this

current mindset supports you to live with passion, work on purpose, and live a fulfilled life. How does it support being an effective leader, and enable you to carry the brand of a leader with which you desire to be associated. How does it work against you?

Hugging Your Adversity

Download the Adversity Gift template from www. alisecortez.com or www.gusto-now.com. It will enable you to make a list of situations or events that have happened in your life, which may have knocked you to your knees and made you wonder what you ever did to deserve them or how you ever survived beyond them. You'll capture your response or reaction to them, then acknowledge who you became as a result and finally consider who you *could* become with a reframing of those same circumstances in a new light – how have they helped you become who you were meant to be?

On the Hunt for Gratitude

For 21 days – the time some say is required to develop a habit – before retiring to sleep each night, write down three things for which you are grateful for from that day. Record them in your journal, which you should keep by your bedside. Also jot down daily even just one descriptive word about how you are feeling. Re-read the journal at the end of the 21 days and see what you notice about the experience, your reaction to doing it, and how you are interacting with others in life.

Bonus Gratitude Exercise

Call to mind someone who once did something that changed your life for the better. Write 300 words, call and schedule a call or visit, read every word aloud, discuss content and how you each felt. Do this – *it will change your life!*

Video: *Meaning as the Ultimate Motivator*

Watch this video at www.alisecortez.com or www.gusto-now.com to reinforce the learnings in this chapter.

2

Identity and Becoming: Your Intimate Dance with Life

If someone randomly approached you on the street and curiously inquired, 'Who *are* you?', what would you say? Does it depend on who asks and how you feel about yourself that day? You will notice a preponderance of concern in this book with forming answers to, 'Who are you?' And 'Who do you ache to become?' The questions will repeatedly be asked through the lenses of meaning, passion, inspiration, and purpose. In fact, you just might find that in the course of the inquiry your identity ultimately is, and always has been, your purpose. It's just that you weren't phrasing it from that vantage point. One thing is certain: you must fully understand your identity in order to be effective in your purpose.

Your identity – that is, how you think of yourself and present yourself to the world – is such a critical aspect of being a leader that its importance is often overlooked. In *The Evolving Self* (1982),[15] Robert Kegan says that how a person settles the issue of what is 'self' and what is 'other' essentially defines the person's meaning-creation system. In other words, the way a person interprets their self and their experience of life *says something about who they are*. The way you think of

[15] R. Kegan, *The Evolving Self: Problems and Processes in Human Development*, 1982.

yourself dictates your stance in the world and how you engage with life. Your identity can profoundly limit your expression of self in the world and who you ultimately become, and it can also unfold into a being you never imagined possible.

That's quite a spectrum of possibilities. As you read each chapter in this book, I invite you to give yourself a space of inquiry to become aware of your governing mindset and any limiting aspects of it, and to cast your aspirations high to 'step into your shine.' In this chapter, I will ask you to analyze your own identity and become present to it in such a way that it is not only malleable but constantly transforming as a project over your lifetime. Finally, you'll learn the importance of telling and recrafting your own story, and get some practice doing so in order to become mindful and intentional about its narrational effects. This will open up new possibilities and empower your future.

So Who Are You, Anyway? Self-Awareness Is Job Number 1

One of the most critical limitations I have observed in my work of training, coaching, and consulting professionals is a lack of self-awareness. Many people simply don't know who they are, and are wholly unaware of how they behave and communicate with others. Because they lack this understanding, they cannot change what they do or how they come across to others, so they are doomed to continue repeating the same errors and missteps in communication, impeding both results and relationships.

To become present to your own sense of self-awareness, consider the power of your self-introduction. I have become sensitive to how I engage new people in conversation, having long ago stopped asking, 'What do you do?' I have found that question limits the conversation, directing it to the domain of work. Since many people don't have a paid job, they may feel a sense of inadequacy when asked this question. I learned instead to ask the new person with whom I'm speaking, 'What do you pour yourself into?' I do it with a genuine curiosity because whatever the person says tells me a great deal about who they are. Whether they go on to say they love gardening, they lavish time on their children or, as in my case, they share a lengthy list of work projects they are juggling at any one time, I've got the answer I was looking for – this person just told me who they are.

The way you describe yourself in social media or in your professional biography also conveys much about you. In mine, I refer to myself as an 'anti-undertaker,' as I am helping awaken people who have been walking dead through life to their passion, inspiration, and purpose. I am a social scientist. I am constantly studying what is meaningful to people, how they understand who they are (their identity), and what motivates them. I am a logotherapist, which is informed by my study and practice in existential psychology and Viktor Frankl's work, which premises that people are capable of and responsible for discovering the meaning of the moment and across their lives. I am also a management consultant, inspirational speaker, radio/podcast host, author, and philosopher. Add in mother, friend, runner, meditation practitioner, ordained minister, and confidante to clients and friends, and you have something of a fuller picture of who I am that distinguishes me for myself.

I encourage you to stay on the devoted path to understanding yourself, which is a lifelong journey. Find ways to introduce yourself that allow you to step into and become more of that person you want to be. A recent example of someone I met who memorably distinguishes himself is Scott Wilson.[16] He makes it a practice to introduce himself as 'My

---

[16] *Working on Purpose* episode 221, Voice America, 5/1/2019.

name is Scott Wilson, and I'm a grateful recovering alcoholic.' This declaration of identity does two things for Scott: (1) its very utterance helps him claim victory over his sobriety and reminds him to continue working toward its maintenance; and (2) it's a statement that grounds him in his new-found purpose and quest to live the life he created in sobriety that eluded him as an alcoholic. Scott has since founded Authentic Success, a business performance consultancy that helps organizations to embrace those uncomfortable experiences with gratitude and grace, helping them to achieve authentic success. Consider how essential it is for Scott to introduce himself in such an authentic way. His introduction humanizes him – it makes him accessible to the leaders and organizations he wants to serve while honoring his own journey.

Form, Function, and Process of Formation: You as a Life Project

Although purpose is your core identity, you will spend a lifetime discovering and unfolding it. Your search for your identity and purpose will in fact *be* your life project – and that will be so for each member of your team. How do you see yourself? Who do you ache to become? Identity answers questions like 'Who am I?' 'Who do I want to become' and 'What holds significance for me?' As I said earlier, what you pour yourself into says something about who you are. You are somewhere along your journey in leadership, whether you aspire to lead a team at some future time or you've been leading for a while and just want to become more effective and inspirational. Your interest in and the way you value leadership are part of your identity.

From my research in meaning in work and identity, I have learned to see the form identity takes as a delightful and delicious stew of at least eight ingredients:

- characteristics or traits
- behavioral tendencies
- values
- skills or talents
- overarching beliefs or perspectives
- goals
- roles
- life-defining events.

For example, one of my traits or characteristics is being extroverted. I haven't really met a stranger and no one is safe – I will approach most anyone and engage them in conversation. Another ingredient that comprises identity is behavioral tendencies. I tend to move and talk quickly, with a lot of energy and 'zest.' This behavioral tendency distinguishes me from people who prefer a more even or moderated cadence of speech and movement. I am aware that I move through the world with a flare of intensity, and I do modulate it downward to connect with people who move with more steadiness.

Values are a key component of identity. I greatly value empowerment, and I live and practice it across my life. It is expressed in hosting the weekly *Working on Purpose* program as my message will almost always have an empowering, inspirational, and educational intention behind it. Skills or talents are other ingredients contributing to our identity. I have a particular predilection for and skill in speaking, reading, and writing Romance languages (Spanish, Portuguese, French, and Italian). And I do take pride in being described by some as 'the little linguist with the radio show.'

Key beliefs or perspectives are another identity ingredient. The way you see the world or your place in it can be a very weighty measure of identity. You wouldn't be reading this book if I didn't hold the strong belief that everyone benefits when they know and live their purpose, which is why I do the work I do helping individuals, leaders, and teams to discover, grow, and live from theirs. For many people, their goals are essential ingredients to their identity. An important goal for you may be rising to lead your department or your company, or found your own one day.

Finally, another major ingredient of identity is contained in the roles we play: mother, father, sister, brother, caregiver, friend, partner, leader, subject matter expert, artist, and political figure are among the endless list of possibilities. Assuming those roles and living out the expectations you believe come with them is a powerful part of your identity. I love being a mom to my seventeen-year-old daughter. I'm so proud of her I could bust. I very much enjoy my role of radio host, as it affords me some essential things I value: (1) as a voracious learner who values ongoing constant improvement, learning, and competency stoking, I get that in spades as I prepare for each weekly program, often reading an author's book in preparation for the show; and (2) those cumulative conversations afford me the role of thought leader in the meaning and purpose category, and I don't take that role lightly.

Through the course of life, many people experience life-defining events that have catalyzed their ongoing unfoldment and development – another key identity ingredient. For some people, their life-defining event is surviving cancer, and this has transformed them into health advocates. Some life-defining events that have helped make me who I am today were living in Spain and Brazil, and traveling through much of Western Europe and South America in my mid-twenties. These tremendous educational and life enrichment experiences helped shape me to become 'a citizen of the planet,' not just an American.

At about this time, you may be wondering why all this navel gazing is important to passion, inspiration, and purpose. It is because identity performs major functions in your life. For one, it helps you differentiate yourself from others, which helps you see yourself as the unique human being you are.

It's also a behavior driver: how you see yourself and aspire to be informs and drives what you choose to do and opt not to do. I think of myself as a thought leader, so I continually scout for distinguished business leaders and subject matter experts to showcase on my radio program so I can learn from them. I look for people and organizations to serve because I am living my purpose to help others discover their own passion and purpose, and then inspire them to pursue them mightily to make a contribution worthy of their one, precious life. Identity can greatly inform how you see your purpose in life, and in fact help you to recognize that your purpose is actually your ultimate and core identity. Stop and read that again. Identity is powerful.

Identity also serves to cohere different aspects of a person. For example, I tend to be a focused and diligent worker (characteristic and behavioral tendency, respectively), and I take pride in creating new offerings and products in service of the vision for my work. I value learning and rely on the catalyzing force afforded to me as a thought leader in meaning and purpose by my weekly *Working on Purpose* radio show preparation. My role as an entrepreneur in the management consulting and purpose category nicely knits these identity aspects together. Can you start to see how your identity 'ingredients' fit together to create *you*?

Now that you understand more deeply the ingredients that comprise your identity and its function, consider the processes of identity. I'll just touch on four here:

1. ongoing life project
2. the stories you tell yourself and others about yourself
3. your own ongoing awareness and development
4. exploration and commitment to new roles over time.

The stories you tell yourself and others are the subject of a segment later in this chapter. Your identity is a lifelong project that will be your constant companion throughout the course of your life. You will be working at understanding and growing yourself over your entire life. Moreover, from the view of Franklian psychology and logotherapy, understanding and embracing the healthy tension between who you are today and who you aspire to be is essential for wellbeing. You will always be 'becoming,' and you will find yourself transformed just by reading this book – especially if you do the suggested exercises, watch the videos, and listen to a few episodes of the referenced *Working on Purpose* radio program. You will always be unfolding. Your call to action is to lean into this process and pursue it with passion, inspiration, and purpose.

The Power of Storytelling: Crafting, Editing, and Sharing Your Story

In the Storytelling programs I have designed and delivered over the years, I offer a three-part approach. It includes capturing who you are and have become; gaining a new and different lens through which to view your life for the better; and inventing a new possibility for the person you wish to live into and become. People are usually hungry to understand their own story – which is a journey of identity-formation. They are also curious to understand what that journey says about how who they are and what distinguishes them from others, and are hopeful about the result.

When you come to realize that how you tell your story dictates the very essence, quality, and trajectory of your life, you will start to realize just how malleable and expansive identity is. The narrative you've constructed of the events in your life has made you into who you are today. It includes all the twists and turns along the way. Who you are and the story you tell are indicative of who you really are at your core, and how you have responded to life's opportunities and inevitable challenges. From a logotherapeutic vantage point, you have the opportunity to recognize that life does not owe you happiness; rather, it offers you *meaning*. Most importantly, the essence of who you are is derived from how you have responded to what life has served up to you and how you have interpreted (created meaning from) those events. Thus, how you make meaning of your life gives you a path to wellbeing or demise – and the response is completely your choice and reflected in the stories you share about yourself.

When participants in my courses do this storytelling exercise, it helps them to take a high-level view of who they are. I'm a fan of the three-sentence model to kick off the process; this renders who you are by declaring what you think of who you are today and how you got that way.

Some examples:

- I am a tortured soul and feel cheated from the life I was meant to claim. I guess destiny has another plan for me. I feel lost and angry.
- I've had just the kind of life I set out for myself to create and was very proud of it. I had big plans for myself and the company I was running. Becoming paralyzed took all that future away from me.
- Amazing upbringing with all the opportunities anyone could ask for. The accident took my mobility, but it didn't take my spirit. I revel in making every day count and impacting as many lives as I can while I'm still here.

Your turn. Consider that the above three examples could very well have been written by the same person. Reflect on what was covered in the previous section about the eight identity components and list those that distinguish you, or stand out as painting color or depth in your life. Next, given some reflection on the matter, consider who you are today, having navigated your life so far? What are you proud of?

Disappointed by? What's the path you're on to become more of the person you want to realize going forward?

The next step requires a conversational partner. Share your story with someone – ideally someone who doesn't know you. Get feedback from this conversational partner: What did they learn about you? What does that story evoke in them? Get feedback on what your partner 'sees' in you through your story. *Hint:* Use the feedback as a way to see how you may want to edit or reframe the events in your story to something bigger, more compelling, less limiting, less judgmental, more forgiving. Doing so opens a space for you to transform to.

The next step of the exercise involves editing. For a proper edit, you need to revisit some key principles of logotherapy. Specifically, logotherapy is an optimistic approach to life that teaches that there are no tragic or negative aspects that could not be, by the stand one takes to them, transmuted into positive accomplishments. Being open to this framing is profoundly important because it embraces the responsibility and power you have to make sense of and classify important experiences you've had – net good or bad. With a logotherapeutic approach, you can always control the attitude you take and the meaning you assign to any events in your life. It is not just an opportunity, but a responsibility, if you want to live life to your full potential.

As you consider your editorial prowess, consider the role of gratitude, which is considered an effective psycho-hygienic tool. Who would you be if those really difficult or ridiculously challenging events hadn't happened to you? Your identity is largely made by what you've given of yourself to the world and how you've responded to what life has thrown at you. Can you summon gratitude for even the horrible events that happened in your life? There's a healing power in seeing meaning in life and all its events, especially if previously perceived as profoundly negative. There are two resources from logotherapy to help you in the editing process of your life story:

- *self-transcendence* – the human capacity to reach beyond one's limited personal interests toward other people, and toward causes that they wish to make their own
- *self-distancing* – the human capacity to step away from one's self and look at one's self from the outside, possibly with a sense of humor.

Logotherapy helps you look for and find deeper levels of meaning in everything you do, and in how you look at yourself. It gives you the opportunity to reframe your life experiences. Consider what have you made of yourself through the life you've lived so far? It is not the *why* of suffering, but the *how* – you can self-transcend and grow beyond yourself. You have the freedom to decide what you will become in the next moment. Standing in that realm of possibility, reframe just one or two elements of your story to transcend to a higher level and claim a more evolved version of yourself.

I have become further convinced about the power of story through my travels and speaking engagements, as I've become something of a 'story catcher' in these interactions. Often, after I speak, someone in the audience will either approach me or send me an email message later, telling me about some powerful aspect of their life that has contributed to who they are today. I came to understand I was 'supposed to do something' with these stories. And thus was born a near-monthly ritual of convening groups (women, men, both) together to host storytelling evenings all over Texas and the other cities where my travel takes me.

An example of an effective and memorable storyteller is Hope Mueller.[17] Our worlds collided when she participated as a panelist on a women's leadership panel I moderated for a pharmaceutical conference in the spring of 2019.

---

[17] *Working on Purpose* episode 235, Voice America, 8/7/2019.

During the course of the day, I learned she was about to publish her book, *Hopey: From Commune to Corner Office.*[18] I immediately understood that her book was going to be a memoir, her life story. The way she tells her story perfectly reinforces the points discussed above, namely that you have complete editorial control over your life story, that it can and does evolve, and there is something you can learn and iterate about yourself as you continue to tell it. Hope's story includes growing up in a commune among adults who frequently smoked marijuana and being largely unguided (but loved) in life and school direction, and moving out to live on her own at age 15. Yet Hope tells her story not as a complaining victim but rather as a grateful celebrant of a full life culminating in fulfillment.

Hope's story and the way she shares it exemplify the power you have in telling your story and claiming with dignity who you have become and made yourself into in response to what life has served up. As you share your story with others and are open to receiving their perspective and feedback on how you've navigated your life, you have the opportunity to grow and transform your identity. It is entirely up to you to exercise your freedom to choose the attitude you take to this set of experiences to make sense of and tell your life story. You also have the rich opportunity and responsibility to determine the life lessons and contributions all these experiences and encounters have made in helping you to become the distinguished person you are today. There is a unique human being that has emerged in you over the course of your life. Can you articulate how your life lessons distinguish you, and are you sharing this unique being to make a contribution to the world? This book was written to get you to say 'yes' to that question.

---

[18] H. Mueller, *Hopey: From Commune to Corner Office*, 2019.

Final Thoughts on Identity

The words you choose and the manner in which you introduce yourself to others can likely benefit from a strong revision or outright recrafting. I'm willing to bet you're not doing yourself justice. Or maybe you are overly smug about who you are, which is equally a problem. How you present and introduce yourself to people you meet sets the course of your unfoldment in life. Though there will always be a continuity thread running through you as you age and navigate life, and a certain coherence of your identity aspects that commingle to make you into the unique person you are today, I invite and encourage you to remain open and hungry for new ways to realize your ongoing identity transformation. Unleash yourself from any limiting, old paradigms and embrace the notion that you can always constantly reinvent and grow yourself into something different or more than you are today.

Your identity is an ongoing life project that *you* get to be the writer and editor of all the days of your life. Keep writing and inventing your story and who you are in it. Your journey as a leader will take you into some very challenging places that will test you to your very core. Don't forget you have infinite reserves to draw from as you respond to those challenges and seek yet more. You'll need to learn how to care for yourself and your team as you navigate your leadership career, which is why the next chapter focuses on caring for your wellbeing.

Key Points and Exercises

Be Mindful of Your Introduction and How You Present Yourself

The way you see yourself and how you present yourself to the world tells people how to treat you, whether to take you seriously, and whether they want to work with you and believe you. To be the effective and inspiring leader you want to become, your first order of business is to craft your identity statement, which can only happen with self-knowledge. Writing helps you gain clarity about yourself. So write two versions: who you are today and who you wish to become. As you read this book and work through its lessons, practice standing and being in that second version – who you wish to become. Pull yourself into that by directing your energies and actions to it. You will be a different person at the end of this book.

Download the Identity Crafting template from www.alisecortez.com or www.gusto-now.com .

Identity as a Lifelong Project

Take stock of your identity using the downloadable Identity Form, Function, Process template to capture the form (ingredients) of your identity, its function (how it manifests in your behavior and choices), and the processes of formation you recognize as contributing to its unfoldment (your life story, new roles, etc.). At the end of the template, answer the question: Who are you? in a few sentences as if you were meeting someone new and really wanted them to know your essence. Download the Identity Form, Function, Process template from www.alisecortez.com or www.gusto-now.com .

The Power of Storytelling

Do this storytelling exercise for yourself and share it with someone who doesn't know you very well. From this exercise, you will start to understand that who you're being, the stories you tell in everyday life, and how you connect all impact the transformative value of meaning you uniquely create and apply in service of your identity and ultimately your purpose across your life. Download the Storytelling – Telling Yours template from www.alisecortez. com or www.gusto-now.com.

Video: *The Ever-Evolving You*

Watch this video on www.alisecortez.com or www.gusto-now.com.

Pay attention to how the choice of language used to describe someone is distinguishing and can empower a direction forward or be entirely limiting.

3

Wellbeing: Caring for the Engine That Powers You

You've heard the term 'wellbeing' used often, but what does it really mean? To help you begin to understand, the World Health Organization (2014) said in a statement:

> *Mental health is defined as a state of wellbeing in which every individual realizes his or her own potential, can cope with the normal stresses of life, can work productively and fruitfully, and is able to make a contribution to her or his community.*[19]

An increasing number of US-based businesses have shifted their focus from wellness programs to wellbeing initiatives precisely because they recognize the importance of a more comprehensive health and productivity program. The offered array includes a focus on the workforce's emotional and mental health, financial education, social connectivity, and sense of fulfillment on the job. In the aftermath of the coronavirus pandemic, Deloitte (2020) issued a report indicating the centrality of wellbeing initiatives, nestled in purpose, potential, perspective, and possibility to enliven and motivate the workforce upon returning back to work after

[19] World Health Organization, *Mental Health: A State of Well-being*, 2014.

the lockdown.[20] In your journey to purpose and becoming a more inspirational leader, you will need to constantly fortify the engine that is you in order to power you onward. To keep your team in high performance mode, you'll need to learn to recognize and monitor their wellbeing and keep them nurtured and fed as well.

Dr Martin Seligman has made a distinguished career in the field of positivist psychology, helping people to access and develop greater levels of wellbeing, and his work informs my perspective and consultative approach. In his book, *Flourish: A Visionary New Understanding of Happiness and Wellbeing*,[21] he distinguishes the aim of positivist psychology as wellbeing, rather than happiness. He declares that the gold standard for measuring wellbeing is to be flourishing, and asserts that the goal of positive psychology is to increase flourishing. That's really worth considering as you continue your own leadership journey and nurture your team members to further unleash their passion and individual greatness. Specifically, Dr Seligman offers the PERMA model that contains the critical elements of wellbeing:

P – positive emotions
E – engagement
R – relationships
M – meaning
A – accomplishment.

I will address positive emotions, relationships, and accomplishment in this chapter; meaning is discussed in its

[20] E. Volini, J. Schwartz and B. Denny, 'Returning to work in the future of work: Embracing purpose, potential, perspective, and possibility during COVID-19', https://www2.deloitte.com/us/en/insights/focus/human-capital-trends/2020/covid-19-and-the-future-of-work.html
[21] M. Seligman, *Flourish: A Visionary New Understanding of Happiness and Wellbeing*, 2019.

own chapter, and engagement is threaded conceptually throughout the book. Being mindful of the state of your wellbeing and constantly cultivating it are essential for optimal psychological health and contribute to improved physical health. When you learn to become and remain in tune with your internal sense of wellbeing, you can more quickly 'right the ship' when you find yourself off-kilter and out of balance, which easily happens among the stress of daily life.

Positive Emotions: Not Just for the Optimists

The world is made up of optimists and pessimists, and I find that most people can readily identify where they fall along the spectrum. Some people take pride in being cynical or sarcastic, often associating this behavior with wit and playfulness. Personal preferences aside, living more often in positive emotions is a clearer path toward wellbeing. The more time you dwell in positive emotions, the more energy or juice for life you can regenerate for yourself and others. Dr Martin Seligman says optimists take action and have healthier lifestyles than pessimists, that optimists believe their actions matter while pessimists often believe they are helpless and that nothing they do will make a difference. Dr Seligman also reports that optimists engage in and benefit from social support, which means you don't have to take on everything by yourself.

Consider the negative emotions of heartache, depression, anger, anxiety and shame, and contrast them to such positive emotions as inspiration, curiosity, fulfillment, enthusiasm, and gratitude. Your emotions are a fueling mechanism that colors and powers your energy, perspective, vocabulary, and way of being. To be a healthy human and an effective leader, it is essential to develop ongoing self-awareness of where you dwell in your emotions. Never take for granted that, in addition to your powerful intellect and rationality, you are endowed with a vast array of emotions that you can spend your life exploring, expressing, and developing. Cultivating your human potential – including your emotions – is vital to realizing your maximum potential and enjoying life to its fullest. Doing so is critical to having the enriching, meaningful relationships that matter in life, *and* registering the impact you yearn to have in the short time you're on the planet.

I've never heard anyone articulate a way to gain access, revel in, and manage their emotions better than Dr Neha Sangwan.[22] Dr Neha is an internal medicine physician and now corporate culture and wellness consultant, among other distinguished credentials. She describes emotions as 'energy in motion,' which means that energy must go somewhere – and she emphasizes the importance of naming the emotions you feel through as wide a spectrum of language as you can to experience them, in order to gain more access to them. This allows you to more deeply experience the richness of the texture and color they add to your life and also effectively redirect them if they register a negative charge for you. So don't limit yourself to saying, 'I'm frustrated.' Expand and search for more of what's behind that feeling. Perhaps you are also disappointed in the person who promised their work in by a certain deadline but missed it, embarrassed that you now cannot meet the deadline for the information promised to your own boss, and resentful that this team member seems to be developing a similar pattern of behavior. Getting present to the 'family of emotions,' as Dr Neha calls them, gives you greater access to understanding and directing the emotions more productively.

---

[22] *Working on Purpose* episode 277, Voice America, 5/27/2020. See also, N. Sangwan, *Talk Rx: Five Steps to Honest Conversation that Create Connection, Health and Happiness*, 2016.

The wide range of emotion is always available to you, even if slowly over time you lost contact with your emotions from your youth. Perhaps life has had a way of 'scaring' them off as you have tried to wall yourself off from disappointment and pain while navigating life's inevitable twists and turns. Maybe you were made fun of for being exuberant, positive, or joyous – seen as 'over the top.' Or perhaps you easily accessed your tears when sad, moved, or hurt – and were labeled a 'crybaby.' But when you allow yourself to embrace your set of emotions, you access a rich intelligence that informs and enriches your life experiences and enhances relationships.

An important benefit pertinent to the message of this book is that experiencing deep positive emotions allows you to be moved or touched – this is emotion at work and a form of inspiration. To be effective as an inspirational leader, you will need to get used to that feeling and allow yourself to be given over to be moved, without restraining it or feeling embarrassed by it. Quite contrary to being embarrassing, when you give yourself over to the beautiful emotions that pour over you and let them color your expression, you and your message are more memorable and stirring. Learn to continue talking beyond the lump in your throat or when your eyes well up as you share a message that is important to you. *Never* apologize for your tears. You've been equipped with this remarkable system that adds so much to the experience of being human – why apologize when they work on you? Let's instead further develop and demonstrate your competence with emotions, which you will learn more about in the next section.

Emotional Intelligence: Your Distinguishing Super Power

By now, I hope you've been convinced to give yourself over to experiencing more of your full emotional spectrum, especially those enlivening positive emotions. Now let's talk about how you can activate, regulate, and manage both positive and negative emotions through emotional intelligence, or emotional quotient (EQ). Increasingly, emotional intelligence has been identified as a key differentiator in leadership. I'll take that one step further and declare that continually cultivating your emotional intelligence is essential if you are to experience life and relationships to their fullest. How you read and take in information about others through your emotions is a critical component to a well-lived and effective life. Whether you are a completely content introvert or an extrovert, you are not only part of society but dependent on it. Cultivating your capacity to read others well, sense their needs and wants, and elicit a meaningful exchange with them will greatly enhance the meaning and fulfillment of your life. As a leader today, or if you plan to become one, developing emotional intelligence is an essential tool.

Becoming an inspirational leader depends greatly on your access to and utilization of emotion. This means getting acutely in touch with your own emotional range and managing your emotions appropriately, as well as helping your team and anyone with whom you interact access, enjoy, and manage their emotions. More specifically, it means allowing registration and expression of your positive emotions to fuel messages of appreciation and possibility for your team members and managing and redirecting negative emotions so they do not hijack your desired results or relationship. Further, helping each member of your team gain greater access and expression of their emotions and coaching them on how to handle the intense ones that threaten to derail their career progress can make an incredible contribution to their ongoing professional development and an enrichment to their lives they won't soon forget.

With emotional intelligence comes the sensitivity to notice when one of your team members walks into your office and is just 'not quite right.' Having sensed the slight change in their demeanor and energy, you can avoid jumping right into the meeting agenda you had carefully scripted, become more present to them, and can ask with genuine concern, 'Hold on, before we get into the agenda, I can see something has your attention elsewhere. What's happening for you?' Your team member now understands that you care about their welfare beyond the job. You may even be able to help with their concern, but even if you can't, you will have made a deeper connection and built a stronger relationship with this person. Everyone has a deep need to be 'seen' – understood, respected, and appreciated. Your use of emotional intelligence just won you some loyalty with this employee, not to mention the benefit of a meaningful relationship. That's emotional intelligence at work.

Remember that you will find yourself surrounded by people who are at various points along the communication skills spectrum. Some will be incredibly astute at articulating their thoughts, and identifying and expressing their feelings. Others will struggle to understand their own internal dialogue and wrestle with converting thoughts and feelings into words. Still others can articulate themselves to others but cannot modulate the ferocity or intensity of their emotions. You, skilled in EQ, can serve as an excellent moderator for them all – helping to give voice and form to some, calming and soothing the ire in others, and being the person that others simply can't resist being around. All in all, it's a pretty good way to walk through life while being effective at leading others to unleash their greatness.

A simple way to start applying emotional intelligence in your life and as a leader is to express and be lifted by positive emotion while handling your natural inclination to react to and be governed by negative emotion. Clearly, the bigger challenge is learning to understand and then calm and redirect your own negative emotions like anger, frustration, and disappointment while helping others to do the same. As your EQ increases, you will develop the ability to express and handle your negative emotions without debilitating consequences for whoever is in the vicinity or conversation. You'll learn to help others gain access to their own emotions and steward them toward a productive use rather than a derailment.

There are two people I'd like you to meet along the emotional intelligence journey, both of whom I've had the distinct pleasure of getting to know through reading their books and having them as radio guests on *Working on Purpose*. Both are articulate, eloquent men of soulful depth who are easy to be around and connect with – indicative of their long-time work to develop their own emotional intelligence. One, Dr Arthur Ciaramicoli, you'll meet later in the book. The other is Dr Sam Alibrando, who helped me to understand how to use emotional intelligence to find your relational 'sweet spot,' the dynamic intersection of power, love, and mindfulness.[23] He explains that human reactivity is the source of most of our interpersonal problems and pain. Think about that for a moment. His book *The 3 Dimensions of Emotions*[24] introduces the concept of working this triangle, a unique practice that provides a compelling yet practical road map that can help you move from painful reactivity to productive proactivity in your relationships. And it works just as successfully for a CEO of a Fortune 500 company as it does for a parent struggling to communicate with a teenager. The key point I am emphasizing here is that learning to manage reactivity in your emotions is one of the most compelling ways to develop your emotional intelligence.

Your success as a leader is largely governed by how well you manage and deepen communication and connection with others, which we'll address next. Learning to understand the source of charge of your positive or negative emotions, and masterfully responding through them in a way that

---

[23] *Working on Purpose* episode 103, Voice America, 1/18/2017.

[24] S. Alibrando, *The 3 Dimensions of Emotions: Finding the Balance of Heart, Power and Mindfulness in All of Your Relationships*, 2016.

increases connection rather than discord, will be an ongoing and progressive journey – but one well worth taking.

Connection and Relationships: Your Lifeline

It doesn't matter whether you work at solving extremely complex, technical problems or take pride in your creative endeavors, we all have one thing in common and that is our need to connect meaningfully with others. At its core, our survival as a human race has largely depended on the ability to stay socially connected to other people. Some psychologists, such as Martin Seligman,[25] suggest that the size of the human brain is partly due to a need to serve social navigation needs. Counselors say it is the absence of meaningful connection in life that most contributes to problems of depression and anxiety. Dr Alex Pattakos and Elaine Dundon assert in their book *The OPA! Way*[26] that in fact there is meaning in life only as long as others need you and you need them. So the quality of your relationships contributes mightily to your wellbeing.

Yet I'm willing to bet that you don't put in the necessary effort or energy to nurture these relationships and keep them strong and vibrant – and neither do I. All too often, we simply don't appreciate a person's place in our lives until they're gone, whether the friendship has vanished, the marriage ended, the teammate left the company, or the person passed away. Given the importance of relationships to wellbeing, even a fractional increase in the amount of energy you give to the people in your life will help produce meaningful results. With the experience of sheltering in place and the

---

[25] M. Seligman, *Flourish: A Visionary New Understanding of Happiness and Wellbeing*, 2019.

[26] A. Pattakos and E. Dundon, *The OPA! Way: Finding Joy & Meaning in Everyday Life & Work*, 2015.

consequent increase in remote or virtual work created by the coronavirus pandemic, this basic human need for meaningful connection has surfaced even more prominently in recent times without the physicality of workplace interaction. You will need to seek novel ways to keep yourself and team meaningfully connected as you lead the way into a future where remote work arrangements will likely increase.

To illuminate the widespread problem of social disconnection in today's world and help you understand the opportunity provided by closing this gap, you need to meet Sharon DeMattia.[27] She is a woman truly on a mission to impact what she has observed as trends of disconnection, which she saw manifesting in depression, anxiety, school shootings, suicide, and war. Sharon found herself stuck in a life of external achievement that lacked real purpose. After a divorce that prompted her to reinvent herself, she founded the AIM Project, a global art initiative about human connection, possibility, and freedom. The AIM Project has a mission to break down the walls people have built within themselves, and between each other, and to open creative, collaborative space on the other side of what we fear. Her creation in the AIM Project involves gathering people across the globe to create anonymous self-portraits that tell a story and help the designers to understand and celebrate themselves while powerfully connecting with others in the group through meaningful dialogue. Let her example inspire new ways for you to nurture more meaningful connection in your relationships across your life and among your team.

Human Agency and Self-efficacy

As you strike out on your journey to unleash yourself from whatever constraints you placed on your life and step into a

---

[27] *Working on Purpose* episode 197, Voice America, 11/14/2018. See the AIM Project website at www.theaimproject.net

new frontier, you will most certainly encounter a wide array of feelings in the new territory. Your level of confidence and motivation to act on those feelings in relation to what you set out to do in your new life are determined by what psychologists call your self-efficacy beliefs.

Let's break this down a bit. Making things happen – translating wishes and thoughts into action – is referred to as *human agency*. Psychologists define human agency as the thoughts and actions taken by people to express their individual capability and power. Human agency is quite useful when considering how to further cultivate passion and purpose across your life, especially when you are out to live your purpose and make a difference in the world. Among the mechanisms of human agency, none is more central or pervasive than a person's beliefs about their capabilities to exercise control over events that affect their lives, a concept referred to as *self-efficacy*. Dr Albert Bandura, a psychologist well known for his research into human behaviour, says self-efficacy beliefs function as an important set of proximal determinants of human motivation, affect, and action.[28] Unless people believe they can produce desired results and forestall undesirable ones through their actions, they will have very little incentive, or motivation, to act; therefore, the results will register accordingly.

Dr Bandura says self-efficacy beliefs are incredibly important to understanding and intervening in people's lives, as they influence whether they think optimistically or pessimistically, the courses of action pursued, the goals set and their commitment to them, the quantity and quality of effort put forth in their endeavors, how long they are willing to persevere in the face of challenges or obstacles, their resilience to adversity, and the accompanying stress and depression experienced as they navigate their lives.

---

[28] A. Bandura, 'Social Cognition Theory: An Agentic Perspective', *Annual Review of Psychology*, 52 (2001), 1–26.

Human agency is exercised through self-efficacy beliefs, which can either help or hinder action. Your behavior is often regulated by forethought in the form of the goals you set for yourself. The stronger your perceived self-efficacy, the higher the goals you set for yourself and the stronger your commitment to them, and vice versa. Further, it takes a strong sense of efficacy to remain committed to our tasks in the face of challenge and inevitable impediments. Fostering an optimistic sense of personal efficacy is enormously useful in life, especially when setting out on a big initiative or chasing a dream.

No matter where you might be on the level of self-efficacy belief toward any one aspect of your life, the good news is that the belief system can be developed, usually in four ways. The first is performance accomplishments. Simply stated, each time you navigate through a new task, you increase your sense of mastery over the task, which in turn influences your perspective on your overall abilities. More successful experiences lead to greater self-efficacy beliefs, and falling short on performing or failing at a challenge can weaken self-efficacy beliefs.

Vicarious experience is the second way to develop self-efficacy beliefs. The simple act of observing someone else perform a task or handle a situation well – especially if the person doing so is deemed a peer or similar to you in some way – can aid self-efficacy beliefs. One of the underlying motivations for me to continue hosting the *Working on Purpose* radio program is to suggest, by way of example, the possibility of listeners enjoying and living lives of passion, inspiration, and purpose precisely by showcasing guests who already do.

Third, verbal persuasion can increase self-efficacy beliefs. Essentially, even simple encouragement by others that you can perform a task or handle a situation will help you develop the belief that you can. Verbal persuasion can take the form of a significant other cheering for you to go ahead and enroll in that class that gets you to the job of your dreams. It can take the form of coaching to encourage and empower the individual to act – something I have had the privilege of doing for years as I coach individuals and groups in the programs I lead. Just like the other three ways, verbal persuasion can also serve to reduce self-efficacy beliefs. Naysayers and other well-intentioned people who remind you of previous failures or tell you your dreams are unrealistic and that you aren't cut out for the life to which you aspire can really drag you down. Beware of who you associate with and listen to, especially as you navigate your path as an inspirational leader working from purpose. Negative people can be incredibly toxic to your delicate and evolving self-efficacy belief system. Balance any negative input you get from them with constructive feedback and skills coaching that will elevate your sense of competency.

Finally, your physiological states are the last area to discuss relative to self-efficacy beliefs and their development. Physiological states include your moods, emotions, physical reactions, and stress response, all of which can contribute to decreasing or increasing your self-efficacy beliefs. Anxiety is often associated with weakening self-efficacy, while excitement increases it. Either way, it is the way you interpret and evaluate your emotional states that determines positive or negative impact on self-efficacy beliefs. You'll learn in Chapter 6 that purpose gives you a crazy sense of energy and courage, and positively redefines your relationship to stress, which greatly enhances self-efficacy beliefs. Disappointments and setbacks can at least temporarily diminish them, and your job is to intervene and remain focused on what you can do, what you want to do, and who you can recruit to help you along your desired path.

One of the best authors and guests with whom I've had the privilege of talking about self-efficacy beliefs on *Working on Purpose* is Rachel Stewart.[29] In our opening conversation to prepare for going on air together, Rachel shared that the major message in her book *Unqualified Success: Bridging the*

---

[29] *Working on Purpose* episode 247, Voice America, 10/30/2019.

Gap From Where You Are Today to Where You Want to Be to Achieve Massive Success was that anyone on a growth trajectory will likely at some point *feel* unqualified for this next level.[30] The aim of Stewart's book is to help readers gain awareness of this important differentiation and then manage any feelings of insufficiency in order to do their work in the world. It's the way she coaches in the book to manage the feelings of insufficiency that I find so heartily celebrates the cultivation of self-efficacy beliefs. The chapter called 'Everything is Figure-out-able' sums up a lot of her message – and aligns with the underlying sentiment of this section of the book. Imagine if you could conjure, in the face of extreme challenge to any goal or dream, the stance or belief that 'I can figure this out.' How would that change your effort, focus, persistence, and ultimately the outcome of your actions?

The way forward toward leveraging positive self-efficacy beliefs, Stewart says, is to embrace the inevitable discomfort you feel in pursuit of your goals *without numbing the feeling away*. Her emphasis is that you must stay in your discomfort and directly confront the three deeply ingrained biological mechanisms of avoiding pain, seeking pleasure, and conserving energy to effectively intervene in your own makeup to grow and further realize your potential. As you confront this discomfort and remain in pursuit of your goals, which also stoke self-efficacy beliefs, you'll have to deal with your co-passenger fear. Stewart coaches (i.e. verbally persuades) so well:

> *Rather than spending all your energy resisting [fear], when it shows up with its extra luggage and its suggested list of annoying detours, you can just recognize that it's a necessary part of your human experience, especially when you are taking your life to a new level. Going somewhere?*

---

[30] R. Stewart, *Unqualified Success: Bridging the Gap From Where You are Today to Where You Want to Be to Achieve Massive Success*, 2019.

Fear's going, too ... But fear never gets to drive – never gets the steering wheel. It doesn't get to give directions, question the route, consult the map, or even control the radio. It just gets to sit in back with its headphones on and go for a ride, hitching a lift with you on the way to your dreams.[31]

Isn't that a wonderful way to quite literally put fear in its place? Fear is a powerful and useful emotion. Stewart reminds us that we must redirect it and manage it in order to stoke self-efficacy beliefs and use fear to channel the hunger to keep pursuing your dreams. It has become so easy in contemporary life, which prizes comfort and pleasure, to quell the hunger and keep it at bay. We do so by numbing it away, as Stewart says, which can take the form of drinking too much alcohol, spending hours perusing social media or watching movies on TV, or any other preferred method of distraction.

A final point I want to celebrate about Stewart's book and our conversation was her statement: 'When we set aside our fears and the many reasons we can't do something as we are unqualified to do it, we progress personally, but simultaneously we lift others and allow them to rise with us. Our unqualified success always has a ripple effect'.[32] This is a perfect illustration of the power of vicarious experience, and it further showcases the point of this book for you. Be the ripple working from purpose and allow it to ignite the same in your team and organization – and make the contribution worthy of your one, precious life. Doing so allows gives you ample opportunity to savor the accomplishments that come along the way, our next topic of discussion.

Getting It Done: Savoring Accomplishment

The master of meaning, Dr Viktor Frankl, says happiness is a by-product of attaining a goal. When people achieve something

---

[31] Stewart, *Unqualified Success*, p 110·
[32] Stewart, *Unqualified Success*, p. 218.

meaningful, they fulfill themselves. I completely align with this perspective, and much of my work is based on Frankl's notion that meaning drives motivation and that the will to meaning is the ultimate motivational force for people. Accomplishing something important to you gives you a motivation to keep going, and in turn you often seek to accomplish something else. In the act of accomplishing something, you get bigger – you grow. Accomplishment contributes to wellbeing because it provides a healthy governing energy that pushes you to realize your goals and what you want for yourself, and keeps you psychologically lifted. You rob yourself of motivation and critical self-efficacy when you put off taking that one simple daily step toward your goals. Righting the path by doing that one thing puts you back on an upward trajectory, maintains a sense of momentum, and stokes your belief that you really can attain the goal.

Continuing to live with an eye on accomplishment keeps you healthy and strong, motivated and persevering through difficulty. It gives you energy. Just reminding yourself that pushing yourself to accomplish what you set out to do gives you more energy to keep trekking on. You will most certainly experience fear and doubt, and sometimes be overwhelmed along your leadership journey. Keep your furnace stoked with belief in your own abilities and motivation to carry you along by staying in continual motion toward your goals. If you are aiming for the next level of promotion or to start a new initiative or company, calendar an event every day and take action on it to help get you there. When you do complete or accomplish something, take a moment to acknowledge and celebrate it. You miss the opportunity to stoke your engine with critical energy when you don't recognize your own accomplishments. Whether it's listening to a podcast about innovation, or founding a new venture, or inviting an expert to an informational interview, use those accomplishments to keep you motivated and on track toward your goals. Of course, you will want to do the same to support those on your team as they pursue their own goals. To aid in the quest for accomplishment, a discussion on mindfulness and meditation will help you see how they enable such pursuit.

Mindfulness and Meditation

The words 'mindfulness' and 'meditation' are often used interchangeably, even though they are distinct. Mindfulness can be considered an ability to be present in the moment, with an open and curious heart, undistracted by other thoughts. Mindfulness is associated with reduced stress and anxiety, increased focus and attention, and being calmer and less reactive. Meditation is an exercise or a way to learn to access mindfulness, and is available in many forms.

Meditation – it's just kind of like napping, isn't it? Well no, as it turns out. Meditation takes place with awareness and consciousness, while napping sends you into an unconscious state. Though meditation is available through many forms, the most important aspect of it is simply to 'quiet the mind,' or give it a place of calm and harmony. This sentence alone should be arresting, given the sheer speed at which life takes place today.

I began my own practice of meditation only recently, in the summer of 2019, after learning about it as a serious practice that can greatly enhance one's life through Paul Skinner,[33] a guest I had on my radio show earlier that year. In preparation for the radio conversation, I immediately became aware that I was dealing with a very enlightened, intelligent man. So when he told me in our initial intake conversation that he meditated and suggested I do the same, I became a quick convert. Though I chose to follow Skinner's lead and practice transcendental meditation, which entails twice daily sessions of 20-minute duration, there are many other forms available. Here are just a few taken from a Healthline article:[34]

[33] *Working on Purpose* episode 229, Voice America, 6/26/2019.

[34] www.healthline.com/health/mental-health/types-of-meditation

- *Mindfulness* – from Buddhist teachings and perhaps quite popular in the West. It involves paying attention to your thoughts as they pass through your mind looking for any emerging patterns. You can focus on your breath or an object as you pay attention to your thoughts, feelings, and bodily sensations.

- *Spiritual* – used in Eastern religions and the Christian faith. It resembles prayer and helps you focus on silence and seek a deeper connection to your God, the universe, or however you conceive a higher order. Essential oils are sometimes used to heighten the experience.

- *Focused* – involves concentration using any of the five senses. Try counting and touching beads, listening to repetitive sounds like a gong, staring at a physical object like moving water or a flame.

- *Movement* – entails movement with thoughtful reflection. Yoga is probably the most common and perhaps considered the purest. But this practice can also be done while walking outside or other forms of gentle movement.

- *Mantra* – uses a repetitive sound to clear the mind. It encourages you to be more in tune and alert to your environment, and to enjoy deeper levels of awareness.

My favorite memory so far in practicing meditation took place in a parking lot. I was on my way to talk with Adrianne Court,[35] the Chief Human Resource Officer at Alkami Technologies, on air about their famous culture. Car doors opened and closed around me. I don't know if anyone observed me and wondered what I was doing – it was not my concern. My practice put me in a comfortable and inquisitive

---

[35] *Working on Purpose* episode 237, Voice America, 8/21/2019.

yet calm state, and Adrianne and I had a delightful, connected conversation afterwards. Meditation really can be practiced almost anywhere and, when incorporated into a daily practice, it can improve your health and increase creativity.

The Right Kind of Tension

As odd as it may sound, comfort is not really a friend. But doesn't everyone strive to become comfortable in life, you ask? It turns out that this idea sounds better as a concept than it plays out in reality. Think of the times in your life when you felt most alive and invigorated. Were they when you were coasting? Seated snuggling on the couch? Effortlessly floating through life? Very likely not.

Would it surprise you to know that a dynamic tension between who you are today and who you strive to become in the future is actually *essential* for wellbeing? As a human being, you need something in your life to catalyze you forward – some kind of internal flame that pulls you onward.

Another way of looking at this is through the psychological lens of 'just-manageable difficulty' or 'just-manageable challenge.' Everyone needs something to strive for in life in order to be their best, to be motivated, to feel alive and well. When working arduously toward a goal – whether it be a college course or degree, getting to the next level in your career, or training to compete in an ironman competition – you are being pulled by that prized next place, which holds an aspirational meaning, otherwise you would not undertake it.

There is a tendency in life to settle into a kind of cadence in everyday rhythms. In the absence of conscious intervention, people merely 'go through the motions' of the days. And that enemy, 'the auto pilot switch,' kicks into gear. That is where the free fall downward gains momentum– it's almost as if life around you starts to play in slow motion and you're sucked into the vortex. This is where people start to fall victim to joining 'the walking dead.' Be careful!

In my work developing leaders within organizations, I frequently encounter men and women who others recognize as successful but who internally feel like frauds or 'imposter gremlins' because they recognize that there is so much more they can be or become. Yet there is some kind of missing element to pull them forward. I often ask them to step away from their current version of life and imagine what could be possible were they to engage themselves more deeply in life. What's usually missing is a catalyst to start the person's engine and awaken them to life's abundant, even endless possibilities. For some, that catalyst comes in the form of navigating divorce, being 'downsized' or 'RIF'd' (reduction in force) from the job, or receiving a scary healthcare diagnosis. Sometimes, those external events or notices can be just what you need to knock you out of your auto-pilot stupor. You can also find yourself radically pulled out of it by inspirational messages or people modeling the kind of authentic life you ardently want for yourself.

Final Thoughts on Wellbeing

You are on a path to develop increasing acumen as an inspirational leader working on purpose. You'll need to stay fit for this kind of life by monitoring and stoking your sense of wellbeing, which registers as vitality. You will know you're living a healthy, passionate life when others remark about the energy you exude in your everyday activities. Descriptors like 'vivacious, spirited, and energetic' will be frequent commentary when others talk about you. That energy emanates from a strong and healthy core and virtually screams, 'I'm alive! Let's go out and play!' It is important to remain constantly vigilant about your state of wellbeing as it can quickly slip away from your notice. Remember, wellbeing includes your whole person – physical, mental, emotional, spiritual, social, professional, and financial. Keeping a finger on the pulse and monitoring it is critical to ongoing self-care and living your best life of passion, inspiration, and purpose.

You might be surprised how tempting and easy it is to ride your emotions from a positive end to a negative one. Raise your gaze to the game you're out to play in life, rather than the vagaries you encounter with people and situations. Remind yourself of the benefit of employing positive emotions while managing the negative ones. Your success and fulfillment as an inspirational leader working on purpose will depend greatly on your ability to continually cultivate emotional intelligence in yourself and in others. Doing so not only elevates the life skills of those you coach toward higher emotional intelligence but also more meaningfully connects them to you. The quality of relationships and your ongoing connection to them are significant predictors of your health and wellbeing, as well as your success at work and as a leader.

That vitality then feeds your self-efficacy beliefs, which govern your agency toward realizing your goals. It becomes an interactive feedback loop in the form of vital tension between your current and desired state that catalyzes higher energy, effort, and commitment to the work. The output that results in achievement is just one of many rewards. When you learn to pay attention to your state of wellbeing and intervene to keep it on a healthy track, life is so much easier and fulfilling. You're no longer pushing the proverbial wet bag of sand up the hill; rather, you have a full tank and are ready to take on life and entertain its possibilities.

Key Points and Exercises

Positive Emotions – Not Just for the Optimists

Note in your journal the positive and negative emotions you experience most frequently. Focus on what you discover, and what it might mean to your ability to live with passion and work on purpose. What is one thing you can start to do to cultivate more positive emotion?

Emotional Intelligence: Your Super Power

Consider your triggers – both those that activate a positive emotion and those that incite a negative one. From the negative list, consider what kind of scenarios or exchanges are associated with the negative emotions, and how you can intervene in your own immediate response to behaviors that trigger these negative emotions to improve communication and connection with the people with whom you interact. From the positive list of emotions, which two or three do you often register? How can you better express them to increase connection in your relationships and team, or elevate someone?

Connection and Relationships: Your Lifeline

Write down the names of the people to whom you feel most connected in life and their relationship to you. Rate on a scale of 1–10 (1 – terrible, 10 – terrific) the quality of that connection. Make a list of the people with whom you'd like to have a better connection in life. For both lists, what is one thing you've learned so far that you can incorporate into how you manage that relationship, which can move up that number? How would having a higher-quality connection to these people add meaning and fulfillment to your life?

Self-efficacy Beliefs

Take stock of your self-efficacy beliefs relative to achieving whatever your next big goal is, whether it's to apply for your next promotion, start a new business, or ask your significant other to marry you. Consider the extent to which your self-efficacy beliefs are positive or negative. Strategize how you can increase your self-efficacy beliefs through performance accomplishments, vicarious experiences, verbal persuasion, and physiological states, as discussed above.

Accomplishment

In the journal you are keeping, record for a week at the end of the day what you set out to accomplish that day, what actually got done, and how you felt overall about yourself each day. Consider carefully what you learn about yourself and how you have the power to intervene mightily in the course of your life. Push yourself to do the next right thing for two weeks and see what happens to your productivity and your mood.

Mindfulness and Meditation

Pick one of the six forms of meditation discussed in this section. Do a little more research into how to do the meditation beyond the introductory information provided here. Pick one and practice it daily for two weeks, if only for five minutes per day. Record any observations about your thinking patterns, your mood, and bodily sensations. Perhaps you can try a different kind of meditation the following week to compare and contrast.

Journaling

Take your trusty journal with you and go spend two hours by yourself, ideally in a place that 'takes you away from it all,' whether that's a local park, a nearby coffee shop, a weekend getaway, or a quiet place in the garage where no one knows to find you. Take stock of the goals you have set for yourself, especially those long-forgotten ones you have shelved. Consider: Why did you give up on them? Are they still important, or have they been replaced by something else? For one or two goals – new or old – that emerge from this exercise, consider some ways in which you can activate a sense of agency to take on the goal. How can you get into that revved-up state that energizes action toward the goal?

Video: *Well-being: Caring for the Engine that Powers Your Life*

Watch this video at www.alise.cortez.com or www.gusto-now.com

What are the key points illustrated that help you recognize that if you don't care for yourself, you cannot adequately care for anyone else?

4

Passion: Your Unique Contribution to the World

When you think of 'passion,' it is easy to default to the glorious feeling you have when you're 'in love' or love someone or something with complete abandon. That may be part of the description or definition, though there is so much more to the term. When I talk about passion, I am referring to the fountain of the energy you give to the world – what you touch, create, move because of the *essence* that emanates from within you. It's almost as if that flame smolders inside you and uses *you* to express this passion. The energy *must* come from somewhere. Passion means it comes from *you* – you give it, like an active service of love, of yourself.

Think of anything you pour yourself into – your kids, your work, your hobbies. Some people say, 'I love to speak to audiences and share messages important to me that I think make a difference to others.' That is an indication of passion for something, and certainly is true for me. When you talk about what you 'love' in everyday language, it's another way of conveying what you're passionate about. The expression or experience of that passion is what you are giving to the world of yourself. When you stand in passion and express it, there is an expansive quality that accompanies it and you are energized. That's a great place from which to live, as it creates a force from within you and makes you compelling to others. Here we have the chief reason passion is so important to cultivate in our lives: it's a critical source of energy.

Living in and expressing your passion actually *gives* you energy. You become bigger in your stance as you express your passions. The energy force field is at work. That is one of the many reasons why living with passion is so critical to wellbeing and enjoying a well-lived life. So when you find yourself low on energy, look for and cultivate things about which you can be passionate on a regular and ongoing basis. Maybe you'd like to join me in taking tango dance lessons or in my ventures in cooking to bring up my game and increase the flavor intensity and creative expression of the foods I cook? In this chapter, you'll learn why passion is a key element in your pursuit of living a full and impactful life, what it means to give yourself over to it in exploration, cultivating and expressing your passion, and how curiosity and hustle are wonderful accompaniments for you.

Suffering and Pain: The Original Meaning of Passion

Sadly, when I'm out speaking to audiences about the importance of cultivating meaning and passion in life, and I ask audience members the question, 'What are you passionate about?', the most common response I get is, 'I don't know.' This reply is often uttered with a stunned expression as this new realization sets in. Human beings are at their best when in active pursuit of something important and meaningful to them. It is in this context that I think of passion as an approach to life, a way of interacting with it that is wholly giving of yourself. When you give yourself over to and live through your passion, everyone you encounter benefits, starting with yourself, brimming with a vibrant energy from within that cascades outward through you and onto others.

It would be remiss to have a whole chapter in this book dedicated to passion without discussing the origination of the word and its underlying tension. The word 'passion' often has religious connotations, such as the 'Passion of Christ' or the 'Passion of the Christian martyrs.' Originating from the Latin root *patior*, passion originally meant 'to suffer or endure.' So passion is not necessarily something that just excites you but rather something to which you become willing to devote yourself. To fully embrace passion requires ongoing commitment and the giving of yourself over to it. You must surrender comfort and endure the pain that comes from giving yourself over to that something. Thus, the dynamic tension you learned about in Chapter 3 is part of what produces the feeling of 'aliveness' often associated with passion.

In contrast, the malaise of today's affluence in many well-developed countries ironically translates to a certain passionless life for a lot of people. The comfort, luxury, and focus on accumulating material possessions that often accompanies 'success' insidiously robs people of passion. You need a certain friction in life to also enjoy growth and joy. It's not that you love something despite the suffering, but rather because of it. So to be passionate about something or someone requires a certain intensity and effort in its pursuit. Passion is energy, and it must be generated from somewhere. It is actually the pursuit of something desired, where the navigation comes with inevitable frustration, discomfort, and pain, that makes you most feel alive.

The book you are reading is absolutely a product of my own suffering in service to produce it. I drafted all but two of the chapters over the course of the last six months of 2018 and then spent 2019 and part of 2020 adding two chapters and further developing my thoughts and ideas, digging ever more deeply to summon words to express what I most wanted to share with you. When I let myself give in to the difficulty of the task and withdraw from my pen and paper (or computer), a terrible malaise set into my being as I knew I was not advancing my cause but rather accepting momentary defeat from its completion. The torture of staying still and focused on this task was maddening, enlivening, exhausting, and then euphoric. A short stint of self-hatred and disappointment would set in until I managed in the next day or so to pick up the task once again. The suffering that occurred between the extreme desire to complete this task and sitting in the awful discomfort of the moment to do so ravaged my soul. And then came a sort of self-generated precious energy that drove me onward. This experience is what I mean by the suffering and pain that accompany passion. What do you feel so intensely about that you suffer from it and are willing to give yourself over to it? Find it! Do it!

What Do You Really Love?

Building on the previous section, let's take this a little deeper. What would happen if you spent just a little more time and energy focused on whatever it is that you truly love? What would your life be like if you devoted yourself to your passion? I imagine you'd have a lot more spring in your step and more people would gravitate to you, wanting to bask in your light. But something happens to people. Over a gradual process, you start to let yourself be worn down by the sheer momentum of getting through everyday life, full of the commute, traffic, a long work day, juggling a personal life and caring for kids or others. And poof, before you're even aware of it, that vital flame has gone out. And then you're in a workshop with me and I ask you that pesky passion question and now *you're* the one with the stunned 'I don't know' reply.

Once you're present to what you love, the next question to ask yourself is how much time you give yourself to dwell with what you love. Doing so fuels you and is a way to express who you are and what matters to you in the world. Yes, you say you love cooking, adventure programs on TV, or [insert favorite activity here], but what are you *doing* about it? A full and rich life requires effort and human agency, giving yourself over in active service to it. It's wonderful that you love something or someone, but what are you doing to cultivate and express that passion?

You probably won't be surprised that it was none other than the rambunctious Roland Haertl, my former boss who fired me, who introduced me to his young grandson, Gavin Doyle, with whom I enjoyed a conversation on air about the very topic of passion.[36] I was introduced to Gavin when he was 17 years old and still in high school, yet this young man had already done so much in life – because he was fueled by an abounding passion: Disney.

See whether you can follow this recipe. Start with one-part loving, supportive, and encouraging family who know how to have fun. Add in one joyful, vivacious kid. Stir in another part tremendous discipline, focus, and determination. Add a dash of entrepreneurial spirit, maybe a little effervescent energy. And what do you get? You get Gavin Doyle, who found his joy of Main Street USA in Disneyland at age four and has cultivated this passion over the years into a very successful business enterprise. Having always had a mind for business, he started with a lemonade stand, later began offering family vacation planning packages to Disney, then created two popular websites devoted to all things Disney. At the time of the interview, he was finishing his last year of high school, applying to colleges, and had just published his first book. Doesn't it make you wonder – what could you do with that kind of passion, and a little inspiration and support in service of its expression? Just imagine what might be possible if you were to help members of your team find and cultivate their passions?

In our on-air conversation, when I asked Gavin where his motivation to do so many things had come from, he mused,

---

[36] *Working on Purpose* episode 32, Voice America, 9/9/2015.

'So, I think, most importantly, it's a fiery passion that I still have for Disney.' He feels a connection with Disney, and Walt Disney in particular, as he believes that everyone has a child within them. At age 17, Gavin uttered words wise beyond his years: 'Everyone's a child that's just grown up. How do we go back to when you were a child, and everything was so simple? How can we make life that much fun forever?' These are indeed very good questions to ponder.

Gavin later began to write about Disney and at one point was writing three new articles a day, all while attending high school. He even had four writers working for him at one point as they gathered and reported news about Disneyland and Disney World on both US coasts. Eventually, that flurry of writing culminated into the writing he was doing when I met him and ultimately yielded his book, *Disneyland Secrets: A Grand Tour of Disneyland's Hidden Details*.[37] In it, he dives into the stories behind the details within every part of the Disneyland Park.

If this early focus and success weren't already inspiring enough, Doyle mentioned casually as the interview continued, 'I think that any business should have a charitable cause behind it. I've always volunteered at a few local shelters and felt strongly my business had to have a philanthropic contribution to it.' So he donates 15% of his book profits to the Make A Wish Foundation, which sends kids to Disneyland among countless other wishes sent into the organization. This is a perfect organization for Doyle to support, and mirrors his own values and way of life. Doyle is an incredible example, from whom any of us can glimpse possibilities for ourselves, to embrace our passion and live with full-on intention.

We can all learn a thing or two from Doyle's example. First, what would your life be like if you worked at nurturing your passion like Doyle did his? What if you helped your

---

[37] G. Doyle, *Disneyland Secrets: A Grand Tour of Disneyland's Hidden Details*, 2015.

kids or extended family members discover their passion and nurture it the way Doyle's parents did for him? And what would happen at work if you helped each team member explore and unleash their particular area of passion? I'll tell you – people would be on *fire*! A big part of being an inspirational leader is helping people get turned on by their lives and work and help them discover their own greatness. Do that and you keep igniting passion and purpose further into the world. Talk about impact!

Employing the Curiosity Tool

What do you suppose would happen if you were to inject *just a dash* of curiosity into your day, your conversations, your own life, the way Gavin Doyle did in his pursuit to learn about Disney? Your curiosity is a way to give something of yourself to the world. It's a way to dance with life in a playful, childlike way. You can look at curiosity as almost the exact opposite of apathy – something to be avoided at all costs, as far as I'm concerned.

I had the pleasure and privilege of teaching in 2015–17 as an Adjunct Faculty member in the Communications Department of Southern Methodist University in Dallas. One of the classes I taught was called Professional Seminar; it was, as I affectionately liked to say, designed to help students 'get and keep their first job.' Of course, part of finding a job is interviewing for it. But before that, you usually need to network and meet new people, putting yourself out there with unknown or intimidating people. Many of these junior and senior students in my class found this part of the course abhorrent, exclaiming, 'Dr C – you're not *really* going to make us go out and *talk* to people we don't know, are you?' To which I'd give a wink and a sly nod, then assign them the task of doing just that – go canvass the city for a place to meet new people. Your secret weapon in this awful crusade?

Curiosity! As I laid out the assignment to go meet three new people and report back what the students had learned about them, I offered these bright and accomplished students a secret weapon that they could employ to make the task more enjoyable and productive: Simply be inquisitive.

The raw discomfort and sometimes terror the students expressed in meeting new people was so palpable that I certainly did emphathize. So I suggested that when meeting someone they didn't know, they should just genuinely lean in and be present with the other person, to *look* for that person. When you peer through the lens of curiosity, you become childlike and the world looks like an adventurous playground summoning your joyous engagement. Opening with such a simple inquiry as, 'What brought you to this event?' can then move on to, 'What do you do for work and where?' And *voila,* you're already on the dance floor and twirling into a fluid dialogue about how your two worlds could potentially and synergistically connect and even manifest into paid work!

For example, let us showcase a young couple from Dallas whose curiosity for making beer has given them a whole new lease on life. Literally. I met Jacob Sloan one weekend night as I was socializing with friends at the brew pub he owns. I was taken in by the passion with which he shared his knowledge of the various beers he had on draft. I prefer the biting, hoppy taste of an Indian Pale Ale (IPA) beer, and Jacob went on to pour a few samples and then regale me with the stories of where they'd come from and how they were made. I was positively enthralled. It wasn't just because on the other end of this conversation was a cold beer. It's nearly impossible to resist someone who can bring you into their world through the intoxicating lure of their expressed passion. Of course, I had to ask how he got into the brewing business, given this obvious love of suds. He replied that he and his wife, Lindsay, had an incurable case of curiosity for the craft of making craft beer. I had to know more and invited them as guests on *Working on Purpose* radio to hear their story.[38]

It all started several years ago when the couple finally put to use a craft beer kit Lindsay had purchased for Jacob as a gift. What began as a curiosity soon became an obsession, and the two found that they loved the recipe development process – collecting ideas, combining flavors, and perfecting aromas in a brew they could call their own. Before long, the home brewery began to overflow out of the spare room and into the kitchen, and that's when the Sloans decided to take the leap and open their nanobrewery and taproom, On Rotation, in Dallas, Texas, serving their own beers as well as a selection of constantly rotating favorites from around the world. Now this zest for crafting beer and coming up with new recipes keeps them going while they learn entrepreneurship and the fine art of running a business. These two young entrepreneurs quite literally turned their curiosity for making beer into a brewing obsession. This begs the question of what your life and leadership would look like if you gave yourself over to your passion(s) and helped every one of your team members do the same.

Passion: Energy at Work

When you stop to take stock of your energy input and output, you will likely become present to a few examples of where you are expending an undue amount of effort with little return. If you are more exhausted than fulfilled in your work, there is an opportunity to 're-work' this situation. The same is true for relationships. Which relationships in your life *give* you energy? Which completely drain you? It is critical that you take stock of your energy inputs and outputs, and begin to ascertain how they are serving you to make the most of

---

[38] *Working on Purpose* episode 16, Voice America, 5/20/2015.

your one, precious life. So much of life is about managing energy – some house cleaning and redirecting of energy will be required on an ongoing basis over the course of your life to live optimally.

Let me introduce you to the 'human sparkplug,' otherwise known as Shawn Anderson, who I met thanks to the radio show. Little did I know that the encounter with him on air would be the spark that pushed me over the edge and into living my purpose! Our initial on-air conversation took place Wednesday, March 8, 2017.[39] That's an important date for me to remember, because the encounter would ultimately change the trajectory of my life for the better. Shawn is all about 'going the extra mile' in life, for digging for what really motivates you and living from that to get the necessary fuel to create the life you terribly desire for yourself.

I wasn't expecting to connect with Shawn as powerfully as I did or to be moved into action the way I was. But his energy, his presence, and his words spurred something in me – and that magic elixir was his passion. By the time I met Shawn, I knew there was more I wanted to do with my life and my work, but I wasn't sure how to proceed. I knew I was stuck in an ineffective mindset and corresponding performance in many areas in my life. I was on the right track, but I needed a different vehicle to get me where I so desperately wanted to go. A few months after our on-air conversation, I reached out to Shawn and tenderly broached with much rambling. 'Look, I know you don't coach people anymore, with everything else you are doing. And I probably couldn't afford you anyway. But would you ever consider … possibly … being my coach?' In his acceptance – and honoring – of this most urgent request, Shawn Anderson has utterly changed my life, which is why I have dedicated my book to him, alongside Roland and my parents.

---

[39] *Working on Purpose* episode 110, Voice America, 3/8/2017.

In my weekly conversations with Shawn, he did for me what others often engage with me to do for them: he breathed life into my dreams by stoking my courage and helping me elicit resources to navigate the journey ahead. In our work together, he helped me become much more present to my own purpose and the tools available to me to honor it and live it on much fuller terms of self-expression. He reminded me of my past successes in order to feel safer in venturing out into new and unknown territory professionally. He urged me each week to set aggressive goals for myself to keep me moving toward realizing what I had set out to do, held me accountable, and expressed disappointment when I did not meet those goals – all of which increased my motivational urgency to stay on track toward the realization of my promises I'd made to myself. It was almost as if Shawn cared more about me becoming the person I so wanted to become and realizing my dreams than I did myself. Never underestimate the gift and power of *you* living *your* passion – and the difference it can make to others.

Get to It: Hustle!

When you think of someone who busily moves through life and prodigiously blows through obstacles and challenges to persist on their path and make things happen, who comes to mind? You, I hope! In pursuit of your aspirations, you need to employ a good dose of hustle to keep yourself on track. By hustle, I mean working with verve, animated by a determination and focus to pursue what you are after in life. Think of hustle as energy intentionally channeled toward a specific aim – so, the expression of passion, squared to purpose.

There's a powerful urgency that comes with hustling. But how do you get it? It helps tremendously to be governed by a fire in the belly that is summoned from being *up* to something important to you. Job number two (after self-awareness, as discussed in Chapter 2) is becoming present to whatever that important goal, job, or mission is for you, then staying present to it and keeping your eye on the prize. By setting daily intentions and declarations in service of this aspiration, you feed your energy to fully unleash yourself to go after that to which you aspire and channel this life-force energy. You can further ignite hustle by continually recognizing that you have only one, precious life that is undetermined in years of life to realize your goals and dreams. Hustle is diluted when you lose sight of that to which you aspire. It is enhanced when you honor the promise you make to yourself to live with passion and work on purpose.

I learned a new thing or two from a conversation with Kate White,[40] the previous Editor in Chief of *Cosmopolitan* magazine and author of many murder mysteries and thrillers. I read one of her books in advance of the conversation in which she outlines nine 'Gutsy Girl' principles.[41] She shared in our conversation how she learned to unleash those instincts that were present in her as a young girl but had been tamped down as she became an adult. White told me that when she was first in New York in the 1970s, she applied for jobs in journalism and wanted to navigate a career that would lead to her becoming an editor. But she was turned down over and often, with the accompanying explanation that women were not allowed to become editors where she was applying.

White also shared how over the years she had to compete with men and lost against them repeatedly. What greatly aided her was her ability to step back and look at the landscape and reevaluate what she had to do differently. She emphasized the continually reinforced importance of asking for what she wanted. She went on to add that part of being gutsy is

---

[40] *Working on Purpose* episode 185, Voice America, 8/22/2018.
[41] K. White, *Why Good Girls Don't Get Ahead But Gutsy Girls Do: Nine Secrets Every Career Woman Must Know*, 1995.

showing your passion: don't be buttoned up, wear your heart on your sleeve about what you want in life, GO for it! She attributes her demonstration of her passion to her success – not being afraid to show people how much she really wanted something she was striving to achieve. To White, hustle is about figuring out your priorities and just going for them. Work your schedule. Dump what doesn't matter. Delegate. Only focus on what's important.

With that kind of singular focus and determination, what could you do with your hustle? Think of the difference you can make, the impact you can have on your team and your organization. You want to do something significant with your life, and you need energy, razor focus, and determined follow-through.

Grit – No, Not the Dirty Stuff Under Your Nails

This living with passion and working on purpose isn't for the faint of heart. It *takes* something to live a life and lead on this level. It takes sustained effort over time and digging deep inside yourself to summon the effort, energy, and fortitude to just keep going. Summoning and then further activating this internal life force is such a vital ingredient to living life to your fullest ability. Although author Angela Duckworth made grit a front and center issue when she published her book, *Grit: The Power of Passion and Perseverance*,[42] the idea has long registered across humanity's history of greatness. The good news is that you already have grit – it's just a matter of developing it as a muscle to help you go after what you really want in life.

---

[42] K. Duckworth, *Grit: The Power of Passion and Perseverance*, 2016.

Grit is a wonderful accompaniment to hustle, and stirred together, the two represent a powerful force. Where hustle ushers in swift and resourceful action, grit summons the perseverance to dig deep and continue on no matter what obstacles emerge in your path. Grit, and its underlying force, work best when you're fully in touch with what it is that is motivating you to work so hard. It means getting palpably present to what you have your eye on. You need to *want* it like your last hope for ultimate fulfillment depends upon it. You have absolutely summoned your own grit throughout your life and known countless others as examples. Let me share with you someone who I think is a living, breathing, walking human billboard for it.

Nancy Shugart's[43] story begins in her early elementary school days when she knew her dream was to become a public-school teacher. There was just one problem: she began to go blind at age eight. Growing up in a small town outside Houston, Texas with only one other blind person in town, she wondered, 'Okay, how do I deal with this?'

The only tool she was given as a small child, with the tiny bit of sight she had left, was a small magnifying glass. When she began third grade, she was bewildered at the thought of reading all of her school books assigned that year. To stay out of the scrutiny of the fellow students who teased her mercilessly about the use of her magnifying glass, Nancy saved all her work until she got home in the evening and only then pored through her reading with that tiny magnifying glass. By the time she got to her teenage years using only this system, and lacking any other understanding of how to cope with her disability, she had become very angry. By her sophomore year in high school, she was ready to give up on everything – her dream to teach, even her own life.

Out of sheer desperation, Nancy began to look around and study people. She began to read biographies, as she saw

---

[43] *Working on Purpose* episode 31, Voice America, 9/2/2015.

them as a roadmap to success. So many of these stories were about someone who had achieved phenomenal success, but whose success she only discovered at the end of the book. She noted the biography contained every failure these people encountered, the struggles they weathered, the mountains they climbed, and it registered for her: 'Wait a minute. They didn't just have it easy and achieve success, they really fought for it and worked for it and were passionate about where they were going, and I thought, Wow! A lot of these people were told they would never achieve success.' She started thinking, 'If people were wrong about these great leaders – leaders of businesses, leaders of nations, leaders of families, leaders of schools, all kinds of leaders – maybe people are wrong about what I can achieve.'

From there, Nancy began to think differently about her life and started to wonder, 'Maybe I too can prove people wrong?' That is when she went to college, and absolutely loved it. But the challenge remained: she was still reading her books with that tiny magnifying glass. By her junior year in college, Nancy was falling further behind, struggling to read all the textbooks. Her Spanish teacher stepped in and quite literally changed her life, suggesting Nancy go to the financial aid office and ask them to hire a reader for her. Nancy was completely astounded, realizing that here she was a junior in college, and no one had ever told her that such a service was available.

Ironically, since Nancy was still able to see a tiny bit, she never considered herself blind, so didn't inquire whether the Texas Commission for the Blind could do anything for her when the agency named was mentioned at the financial aid office. Upon visiting with a representative from this Commission, Nancy showed her the letter from her ophthalmologist that she had received 12 years earlier indicating her visual acuity to be 20-200. The counselor told her that this result indicated she was legally blind, to which she replied 'No I'm not.' After a volley back and forth of 'No,

I'm not,' and 'Yes, you are,' Nancy was astounded to finally understand she had been blind for 12 years and didn't know it.

In the course of that conversation, Nancy learned of a machine in the university's library called a CCTV, today called a 'video magnifier.' The counselor sent Nancy to determine whether the machine could enlarge the print sufficiently to permit her to see it. The librarian put her in front of the 'video magnifier,' which looks to the rest of us like a large television screen that sits on legs. Nancy pulled out her music history book, opened it, and placed it under the machine; she immediately realized the machine could raise the print by about 40 to 60 times – well beyond anything the tiny magnifying glass she'd been using for the past 12 years could do. She broke down crying, bowled over with the sudden and intense realization, 'I know I can do this now. I can finish my college studies. I can become a teacher.'

As Nancy narrated her story and I listened with tears moistening my eyes, I finally asked her, 'Why be a teacher?' She replied:

> *I don't know if it's just something that we're born with, this passion in our heart, but I just knew from the time I was five years old that was what I wanted to do. But, for me, it revealed itself very early. I wanted to make a difference. I would picture myself up there in front of the students and thinking, 'I want to make learning fun. I want to get through to every single child.'*

Nancy refused to give up on her dream. Today she is retired from decades of her beloved teaching, and is an author and speaker; she also runs her own company. Her platform and book, entitled *Prove Them Wrong*,[44] are designed

---

[44] N. Shugart, *Prove Them Wrong: The Kids Who Refused to Quit*, 2011; www.provethemwrong.com/about-nancy-shugart

to provide unshakeable evidence that we can all do more than most believe to be possible. Everything about Nancy Shugart exemplifies grit. If she can access it, so can every last one of us.

Final Thoughts on Passion

This chapter is a reminder that to live a life of passion requires giving strongly of yourself and constantly embracing the tension that accompanies the giving over of yourself to what you love. You *need* that tension or friction to generate energy in your life, and I hope you recognize now that without that tensional force you will fall prey to walking dead through your life, completely missing the opportunity to lay full claim to your one, precious life.

Discovering and cultivating what you love – that is, finding those areas of interest or persons to which you feel strong emotion – is essential to living with passion. There is so much in the world that needs your attention and love – there is no end to the problems the world has that need your passion to solve. Employing a childlike curiosity in everything you do not only expresses your uniqueness but gives you access to discovering more connection, possibility, and even greater passion.

Living with passion takes a good supply of energy, which you must guard and fortify mindfully and intentionally. Choosing which activities and persons to opt into and out of is key, and nourishing your life with energy-infusing contributions makes all the difference to living and working with passion. Fueled with that energy, you are better positioned to hustle to keep up a good pace in pursuit of your goals and dreams. Success and financial comfort can present strong deterrents to challenging the comfortable complacency that comes along with them. You will need to cultivate your grit and lean on it heavily to get you through the inevitable roadblocks that life will present – see them as its way of checking whether you're really serious about that dream and about growing into the leader you aspire to be.

Never forget that what you give of yourself to the world in the way of these passions, it gives you back many times over. The more you put of yourself into the world, the more you enjoy an increased return on investment back into yourself, refortifying the whole process and system. In the next chapter, you will learn where passion and inspiration meet and how they synergize to thread energy across your life.

Key Points and Exercises

Find Your Passion

Identify one or two things you're passionate about. The list can comprise activities, hobbies, a field of study, a person, a cause, etc. Make one item on the list something related to your work or leadership (as in my example of recognizing or elevating people, something I do in my work and everywhere across my life). For anything you place on the list to qualify, you must 'pour yourself into it' – give yourself over to it. Consider why you love those things, and how giving more of yourself to any one of them could enhance your energy and vibrancy in life.

Look into Your Past

Think back – what were you passionate about as a child? What positively captivated your attention? It may not indicate anything that can be channeled today, but take yourself back in time when passion registered. Can you thread a passion from back to your childhood? Do you still 'permit' yourself that passion to be expressed into and through your life? How so? Or, if applicable, why not?

What Do You Love?

What do you love? What do you throw yourself into? Does it relate to or involve what you already do for work? How so? Why not? What could you do to draw from what you love more deeply in your work and leadership? What do you wish you would have done had you had the chance? What does someone in your life show enthusiasm for that you could encourage?

Curiosity

What were you terribly curious about as a child? What could you not put down? Are you still curious about it and do you still put effort to it? An enduring curiosity can be the seed of passion and purpose. Do you set aside time and effort to dance with this curiosity today? Why or why not? How might your life be different if you gave yourself over to that curiosity just a little more each week?

Priorities

Identify one urgently important priority in your life or work. How can you alter or rearrange your schedule to give you more focus on that priority? What do you need to dump or put on the 'I'm not doing this right now' list in order to bring a determined focus and commitment to that priority to activate your hustle? Standing in the place of having accomplished this priority, how can you channel that accompanying success energy to pull you forward in daily focused activities?

Grit

As we have all practiced grit across our lives, take a moment to recall specific instances where you have witnessed it in action for yourself. What was it that was calling you to pull from this well of energy? What were you ardently wanting or striving for? Why was it so important to you at the time? Now, in the present day, what do you hunger for in your life that is leaving a vacuum in you, but that with a good dose of grit would pull you to its realization?

Video: *Passion: Your Unique Contribution to the World*

Watch this video at www.alisecortez.com or www.gusto-now.com

What are your key takeaways to fortifying passion and its expression in your own life? What new ideas present themselves to help your team members access and develop their own passion?

5

Inspiration: Breathing Life into Your Being

Where *passion* is what you give of yourself to the world, *inspiration* is what you get from it. You need only to be open to the wonder and awe that is everywhere around you to harness your talents for discovering meaning in those moments. I like to think of inspiration as anything that fills your tank, washes over you as 'goodness,' or moves you. From the original Latin root, *inspirare*, the word 'inspiration' literally means 'to breathe into.' Thus, you can think of inspiration as breathing a certain life or life-affirming energy into you and others.

Good news: if you're not currently totally turned on by life and inspired by the wonder in it, it's there – you simply need to go looking and become present to it. You can always employ your new friend, curiosity, who you met in Chapter 4. But if being present to inspiration is not your natural proclivity, you'll need to cultivate and exercise the muscle of looking. Start small and simple. Read short snippets from your favorite news source – who's doing something that makes the world better? Listen to my weekly *Working on Purpose* radio program – I consciously source guests who advance the conversation on living with passion, working on purpose, and doing business mindfully.

Go on an outing or adventure that lets you step into a new kind of wonder. I don't care if that means you and your family take your first tram ride into some new part of the city – but go looking into the world with fresh, curious eyes as to what and who can be discovered that just inspires you to want more for yourself or give more of yourself. At work and with your team, what new great idea did you hear shared in a meeting that could really make a difference to your business? Do you admire the creativity or the intricacy of the plan? When you bear witness to that act, be there – present in the moment – and let it wash over you. Let the feeling of humans caring for each other, or just being great, make a deposit into your heart.

Learning to access and be transformed by inspiration is one of the critical tools in your toolkit as you navigate your journey to purpose and develop yourself as an inspirational leader. In this chapter, you'll gain deeper access to the plentiful resource of inspiration. You'll learn how to access it more fully through your senses and embrace possibility as a conduit to inspiration. Cultivating the emotion of 'awe' may sound bizarre at the outset, but you will learn how it opens a wide path that stokes inspiration. And when you allow inspiration to work its magic on you, I'm asking you to give yourself over to it and let it quite literally *move* you to a higher plane of consciousness. You've set out on an ambitious path, and you will need a constant infusion of energy and possibility to fuel you onward. The more you build your capacity to experience inspiration, the bigger the space you create in yourself to sense more and cultivate it for others. I promise you'll find more energy, be more grateful, and be more in touch with your fundamental life source.

Be Inspired – It's an Action Verb

Living with and allowing yourself to be elevated by inspiration is greatly enhanced when you develop a certain predisposition to inviting openness to the world around you. I'm asking you to cultivate this sense along the same habitual level you've developed to brush your teeth, take vitamins, drink water, exercise, and sleep. It's *that* essential to wellbeing. Living on this level entices you to step outside of yourself, your own world of whatever ails or preoccupies you, while meaningfully connecting with the world around you. In other words, you are well served when you embrace inspiration as an action verb across your life and actively live it.

Cultivating the senses is a great place to start feeding inspiration. Appreciating the wonder and beauty of a spectacular sight and experience of sunrise in an active way is a great place to start. Go on an inspiration hunt – I promise you can find it. My South African friend Henda frequently invites me to join her to watch the sunset at White Rock Lake here in Dallas. There is something magical about experiencing the sunset with her, someone who grew up with the sun being such a strong orientation in life. We often catch up on our lives together and watch the sun slowly descend into an orange drop from the sky, and marvel at the clever way physics and nature take such good care to ensure this phenomenon occurs every day.

To gain access to inspiration, let's take a brief tour of our senses – starting with hearing. There's a reason I host my weekly radio show and am enthralled with and speak a few Romance languages. The richness and full array of the human voice elevates me. I pay attention to how people speak, their accents, and the way they choose their words to express themselves. Any accent outside the United States is also compelling – it says to me, 'You're different than me, let's talk, I want to know you!' I can speak and write Spanish and Portuguese in a conversationally comfortable manner, and I have some utility in French and Italian. I also learned about 25 words of Tamil (one of the 21 official languages in India) during my trip in December 2014. You get the idea. I stoke my hearing sense every chance I get to let its contribution wash over me and feed my soul.

Smell is an accentuating sense for me – it just adds a nice touch to everything else. Opening the jar of fresh cardamom pods I got from New Delhi, India some time ago, and taking a whiff of them, can completely change my day in one instant, always for the better. Their deeply fragrant, intensely spicy scent catapults me to some other distant land as I take leave of the confines of the moment. This is a spice I always have 'at the ready' in my home – for creating tasty and divine meals, and for a simple 'pick me up' drive-by smell as I power through my day.

Taste. Yes, I am one of those people who can have a *When Harry Met Sally* moment[45] in the diner. Hands down, my favorite food to eat for flavor is Indian, as I find the intensity and complexity of the taste tantalizing. I don't eat it frequently, though, because doing so would easily result in a couple more dress sizes as I'd consume more calories than needed to sustain myself. Thai food is my go-to for good spice and grounding in protein and vegetables (my waistline is also safer).

Touch is another very powerful sense for me. As I sit writing these very words on a beach in Cancun, Mexico, there is a gentle breeze gracing my hair, swirling gently over my skin. It's so pleasant, so enlivening. Feeling it makes me appreciate that I'm *alive* – I have access to and have been granted this amazing sensation. Letting the world pour over you by inviting it in is the beginning of inspiration.

To find inspiration, you need only look for and proclaim the wonder in your everyday life. Those moments and experiences are everywhere across the day, if only you know how to be present and look. You might think of inspiration as a way to pay homage to this wonderful thing called life. It means walking in appreciation of the marvel around you, letting its sensation wash over you and expressing what the

---

[45] For information about the movie *When Harry Met Sally*, see www. imdb.com/title/tt0098635

experience evokes. Passion requires energy, and inspiration helps you to fuel its expression.

Relationships and the everyday experiences you have with people serve as powerful reserves of inspiration. While speaking at the Asia HRD Congress in Kuala Lumpur, Malaysia in August 2017, I had the remarkable good fortune to cross paths with fellow speaker Kimo Kippen.[46] Kimo exemplifies inspiration as he takes gratitude to a whole new level. In his presentation, he spoke of the opportunities he enjoyed at the helm as Chief Learning Officer and Vice President of Global Workforce Initiatives at Hilton. His words were uttered well beyond a place of appreciation, on a higher plane of inspiration, as if he were standing in the wonder that this life, *his* life, had been bestowed upon *him*. He was truly inspired by the life he'd had the privilege to live in his long career, and has since retired from corporate America to continue consulting on his own. As Kimo shared other breathtaking aspects of his life, he was moved to tears when recalling fond memories of his parents. He transported himself from gratitude to inspiration in recalling how much his parents loved him. It was incredibly powerful to be in the audience as he narrated his experiences, and I dare say that each of us were moved to a higher plane as he brought us into the world as he so uniquely experienced it. Your opportunity is to continually open yourself to experiences and observances that, when you fully experience them through your senses, fill your tank with meaning-infused energy, served up in the form of inspiration.

Inspired by Possibilities

To be inspired by possibilities effectively requires that you suspend what you currently believe to be true or possible,

---

[46] *Working on Purpose* episode 156, Voice America, 1/24/2018.

and open yourself to transcend these limitations. When you do, the world around you literally pulls you into a higher state, a more energized realm. Following the news today, you may be tempted to fall prey to sarcasm and cynicism that the world is going to hell and a handbasket. But that is so untrue – even in the midst of the COVID-19 pandemic that was plaguing the world at the time of this writing, there is still an enormous supply of kind and generous people performing extraordinary feats and service, giving their time and resources to help others. People in communities are bringing food and clothing to neighbors who've lost their jobs and are struggling to make ends meet. Companies are diverting resources and cutting executive pay to ensure more employees can stay on the payroll during the downturn in the economy. What would happen if you focused more on those individuals and companies than the ones who make the news with their acts of hatred, crime, and terrorism? How much life could you breathe into yourself and others by standing on that platform instead?

It is easy to give yourself over to getting caught up in the pace of everyday life and focusing on limitations or boundaries. The sheer speed at which life presses on can be overwhelming. I hear people in my leadership programs say all the time, 'Oh, I couldn't possibly do _____,' usually followed by, 'I just don't have enough *time!*' Fill in the blank with whatever activity, adventure, or scenario you wish. When your view of the world is contained inside a box or frame, you entirely miss all the contents outside the confines of that container. Here it can be helpful to go back to mindset and the importance of cultivating one of possibility rather than one viewed through a lens of limitations. Yet how often do you venture into that vast world of endless potential and let yourself marvel at the wonder of what 'could be' for you or your team? Please don't ever stop dreaming – you need the pull of its possibility to keep you vitally inspired and unleashed toward living your life to its fullest and taking your leadership to its peak.

Consider the myriad possible scenarios for yourself. Standing outside the realm of your current existence today, what do you cast your gaze toward as desirous? What if you started not with 'I can't do X because of Y' and instead considered 'What can I do or summon today that gets me closer to X?' And 'Who might be able to help guide me in my quest for X?' Brainstorming a list of possible scenarios to help move you closer to your prize opens a door beyond what you're certain is possible today.

It is so important on this inspiration and purpose journey to seek out people whose speaking or writing tantalizes you. Examples abound and are everywhere – you need only pay attention to their message. I found myself thoroughly elevated by speaking on air with Karen Hoyos,[47] a firecracker of a human and global transformational figure focused on helping people across the globe discover their purpose. In her book, *Purpose: The Ultimate Quest*,[48] she states that currently only 1% of the world's population are fully living their purpose. Prepare yourself for this: She goes on to say that when we reach 3% of the world doing so, human consciousness will be raised to such an extent that *peace is actually possible.*

Now, that's worth getting up for! That possibility inspires every fiber of my being! I'm IN! I'll devote myself to helping as many people as I possibly can in the days I have on earth in service of this task. I know that everyone wins when a person finds and lives their purpose – their significant others, their children, their communities, their employers, their team. Now, when you add the prospect of achieving world peace, that possibility stands as a beacon in the sky pulling my every force.

While this possibility of peace is just a singular source of inspiration, it happens to be shared by Dr Kathleen

---

[47] *Working on Purpose* episode 219, Voice America, 4/17/2019.
[48] K. Hoyos, *Purpose: The Ultimate Quest*, 2019.

Kuehnast,[49] who I got to know on air in October 2015. She is the Senior Gender Advisor at the US Institute of Peace, and I crossed paths with her when she was in Dallas to speak at a conference I attended. She shared with me how serendipitous interventions in her chosen career path yielded surprising and completely unpredictable results. Dr Kuehnast was set for an academic career in anthropology but found herself in the middle of a crisis situation while working on her dissertation in the post-Soviet country of Kyrgyzstan. Setting aside her academic aspirations, she accepted the call to action from the World Bank to help Muslim women adapt to the complex social and economic changes during the post-Soviet transition in the 1990s. This single act would set in motion a full and ongoing career in international development, unification of gender interests, and helping people in conflict to work toward peace. Overall, her work has been focused on the UN Resolution 1325 and the critical role that women should play in all aspects of peacebuilding. Dr Kuehnast's work is a reminder to be open to unplanned opportunities in career paths – and to recognize that each and every one of us can be everyday peacemakers, or impact the world in a way that vitally matters to us, if only we embrace the possibility of that inspiration and choose to lean into it.

Authenticity as an Opening to Experience and Relationships

Authenticity starts with being brutally real with yourself, about yourself. Consider how much of your life you may have tried to shield yourself from your own view, to hide from your past or cower from your potential light. To spend time in inquiry about who you really are and what you stand for takes

---

[49] *Working on Purpose* episode 39, Voice America, 10/28/2015.

some real work and a heavy dose of courage, as discussed in Chapter 2. The journey usually instills a sense of humility as you learn how much you have pretended or simply chosen not to see about yourself. You will need to learn to trust that the raw authenticity that leaves you bare, exposed, and vulnerable to the world's touch will handsomely reward you with the rich experience that accompanies it.

Think of authenticity as being true to your personality, values, character, spirit, and emotions. I'll bet that at various times in your life you've probably struggled with letting people at home or work see you for who you really are, for fear of embarrassing yourself, being rejected, or being ridiculed. Living with inspiration takes real courage to allow yourself to openly connect with people and experiences, and let in the emotional tide that often comes from allowing yourself to 'touch the light' of these rich and deep interactions.

What's the payoff for being authentic? It's a fantastic connector tool that helps considerably to open and develop much more meaningful everyday encounters and relationships. Authenticity is a quality that can be constantly cultivated and grown; when employed, it draws people irresistibly to you as they sense the presence of your veracity and accompanying tender vulnerability. Getting to the place where you can harness this magnificent resource means doing the work of getting in touch with your very essence, your soul, and then sharing it as wholly as you can.

In my many exchanges and interactions with people courageous enough to put themselves out there in the most real way, and register profound results, I can think of few I've crossed paths with who have done it quite as well as Dr Cary Israel.[50] From 1999 to 2015, Dr Israel served as District President at Collin College, a multi-campus operation serving more than 53,000 students annually in north Dallas. Under

---

[50] *Working on Purpose* episode 266, Voice America, 3/11/2020.

his leadership, the college was nationally recognized for its outstanding and innovative programs. But from the outset, Dr Israel encountered a constant onslaught of naysayers – people who severely and often publicly questioned his leadership decisions and initiatives.

Leading from authenticity means being true to your values and purpose. One of the things Dr Israel did early in his tenure was to raise the pay of his staff and teachers on par with prominent universities like Brown. Being an inquisitive and mindful leader, Dr Israel became aware that many of his staff and teaching team were on food stamps or worked a second job or two to make ends meet, an economic disadvantage he felt compelled to address. That decision was just one of many that brought ire from various stakeholders, though he stood behind it so staff could focus on serving the students rather than making ends meet.

Dr Israel shared with me on air that he knew he was not a popular president in his years of service, though he was proud of the results he and those with whom he worked were able to deliver. He remained true to his values and purpose that he was optimally serving the students and community of Collin College and followed through on his decisions accordingly. Imagine the courage it took to stand in such vulnerability. Yet the results speak for themselves – Dr Israel's legacy will live on for decades.

Do you think you can lay bare your values and purpose to deliver on your leadership, and make the difference worthy of your one, precious life? To activate the requisite courage to be this authentic and vulnerable, you will probably need to confront some hefty challenges that rattle you to your core and require an emboldened response. Dr Israel was challenged on numerous occasions regarding his decisions and desired direction, but what kept him on track to follow through on his values was an unwavering belief that he was serving the highest value and greatest number of stakeholders. Once you hit a threshold like this, and push yourself to persevere through it, you will come out the other side bigger, bolder and more capable to take on the *next* challenge.

What Moves You?

What is it that stirs you deep inside? What causes your emotions to well? What is that gives you a lump in your throat? Another way to say it is by asking what moves you. For some people, it's hearing their national anthem being played – which results in deep feelings of pride, honor, and loyalty being called forth. For others, seeing a beautiful opera performance may stir and move them. Watching your child face their fears and stand up to perform in the school play and just nail it – the pride and joy that experience produces can move you to tears.

To play full out in life is a full contact sport. The opportunity is to *allow* yourself to be fully present in these moments, fall into them, let them wash over and overtake you. Are you one of the many people who have hardened over time and become more resistant to giving yourself over to these beautiful moments and experiences? Do you guard yourself, holding yourself stiffly so as not to let your tender emotions show, lest you become vulnerable to others and seen as 'weak'?

In my work conducting purpose-inspired leadership programs, I see participants gird themselves strongly so no one sees their emotions. Women especially are often reticent to show emotion in the workplace and let themselves be moved, because they have been told for so long to contain and control their emotional life in order to be taken seriously by men. In the public workshops, and when I work with women only, this is not the case – they openly and powerfully express their emotions in the comfort and safety of fellow women. Men I encounter working inside companies are often more open and less fearful to show when they've been moved. Perhaps it's because they have finally broken free of the messaging so heavily imbued in their youth to 'be strong' and 'don't cry', and they haven't been punished in the workplace for registering the powerful compliment of emotions as many women have. At any rate, let's restore humanity to its fullest in the workplace and at home – *vive émotion!*

There are many occasions that make the list to move me, but for the sake of brevity let me restrict this example to cinema. I want to open a space of inquiry and possibility for you to expand the arena of just how abundance can move you in your own life, and certainly as a leader, when you allow yourself to fully experience inspiration.

Recently, my daughter suggested I see the movie *Five Feet Apart*, starring Haley Lu Richardson as Stella and Cole Sprouse as Will.[51] It is based on a true story about two teenagers who meet in a hospital where they are being treated and trying to live with cystic fibrosis. Hospital rules state that they must remain five feet apart (hence the film's name) to keep their compromised immune systems from being in contact with others and risking life-threatening infection. I was tremendously moved by the powerful dedication Stella had to sharing her story and educating her YouTube followers on cystic fibrosis. I was also moved by the discipline to her own school studies while in the hospital, despite her treatment regimen. It is such a testament to the human spirit to persevere and practice discipline.

Will and Stella venture out of the hospital on their quest to experience the evening lights, unprotected and out of their hospital cocoon, representing a desperate effort to embrace life at the potential (and likely) cost of infection. I found the outing romantic, and it moved me to tears, considering that I would take a simple outing like that so easily for granted. But for them it was a life-risking undertaking. In fact, Stella falls through the ice in a pond during their outing, and Will rushes in to save her by pulling her from the ice-cold water

---

[51] See www.imdb.com/title/tt6472976 for more information about this movie.

and performing the dreaded touch through mouth-to-mouth resuscitation. This scene elevated my soul by witnessing the beauty of loving someone else so much you no longer consider your own life.

Back at the hospital after this scene, when Stella was finally in a position to receive lungs from a donor, and he wasn't qualified to be on the list, Will begs her to take them in order to live, knowing his own days are numbered. This kind of beauty, when I observe it, transports me to a higher level of what it could be to exist in this life. And that inspires me! It gives me wings, makes me bigger, and makes me want to be better. And that's what this whole chapter is about. Inspiration gives you juice, wings, possibility, and energy. It expands you. You need that to power you through living and leading the life of passion and purpose you want.

Your work as an inspirational leader will naturally and increasingly have you present and responding to what moves you. As you witness a new team member jump out of their comfort zone to give the department presentation they were so nervous about, you might find yourself moved by their courage and dedication to you and the team. Your opportunity – and, quite literally, your job – is to let your inspiration show. Let this person see how their courage moves you. Tell them how impressed you are with what they have done to break through their fears and help the team. Doing so will create a powerful connecting force and elevate you both. The major bonus is that it also goes a long way towards increasing this team member's motivation to work with you and stay on as a follower.

Creativity Can Come from the Most Surprising Places

Do you consider yourself creative? Or, does this adjective only apply to other people? For the vast majority of my life, I emphatically denied having an ounce of creativity in my being.

I staked claim to the pronouncement, 'I am NOT creative' almost defiantly, as if to distinguish myself. It probably started back in my art class in middle school where we made pottery. I still remember the grotesque formation that was supposed to be an ashtray and I wince at the memory (yes, back in the 1970s we still made those in school).

Fast forward many decades ... Occasionally, over recent years, people would remark, 'You're *so* creative,' to which I would react in complete astonishment, 'What are you *talking* about?' And under my breath, I'd say, *what a poor, misguided person* – thinking *I'm* creative. I found the comments so perplexing, and I dismissed them as having come from someone who surely was deranged or simply couldn't possibly understand creativity themselves. Yet I remember so clearly when I finished my research on meaning in work and identity research for my PhD dissertation and found (then) five modes of engagement for the participants. One keenly wicked smart committee member, whose learned opinion I greatly valued, remarked with affirmation and appreciation, 'Your work, approach, and methodology are very creative.' I think it was her utterance that began to change the tide on my limiting view of myself and led me to begin to accept my capacity for creativity.

My investigative research for that project was done entirely from a place of inspiration. The world of work inspired me to my core – and still does. After all, at the end of the day, how you walk through life is intensely governed by the work you do if not for the sheer force of time you devote to it. The 25 men and women managers working in IT who I interviewed for the dissertation inspired me to reach deeply into their experience of work (which I thought was hugely important as IT perpetually changes the way healthcare is practiced, communication is practiced, and transportation takes place, among many other applications). I wanted to understand how *they* experienced their work and what it meant to their sense of self or identity. *That* inspiration fueled my research and filled me with a sense of *mission* (which differs from purpose, by the way – mission is *what* we do in service of our purpose). That inspired mission gave me a space from which to create.

Later, I would summon that same inspiration to greatly expand the initial research from 25 participants in IT to 115 men and women across 20 different industries and between the ages of 18 and 78 to understand how they experienced meaning in their work and the relationship to their identities to find 15 modes of engagement. Inspiration is an incredibly important component of creativity. I invite you – urge you – to give way to your passions, to let yourself be inspired by your everyday experiences and surroundings. You might just astound yourself with your own creativity and what you can bring forth to the universe. We're ready. We need it. *Bring it!*

In my work consulting with individuals and organizational leaders to help them discover and grow their purpose and cascade it across their lives, I have come to see that creativity can be summoned from a purpose-lens. By that I mean that how you see the world, its opportunities, and your ability to contribute to or impact it is uniquely construed through the lens you apply, as obtained through your purpose. I have had an unyielding fascination with how people engage themselves with the world through their work. That is my purpose-lens. That unique lens is what allows any creativity to pass through me as I intensely look for what's possible within people through their connection to work – which is such an enormous part of life. My drive, passion, and inspiration connected to purpose open a window for me that lets me see the unique connection people have to their work in a fresh way that few others have yet considered.

To showcase how creativity can show up in interesting and perhaps wholly unexpected ways – and as innovation in organizations – meet Bob Benkowski.[52] Our conversation celebrates the wonders of youthful curiosity and fascination.

---

[52] *Working on Purpose* episode 101, Voice America, 1/4/2017.

I share this particular conversation as representative of creativity precisely because Bob took the lens he learned from his work in aeronautics and applied it to medicine, yielding something completely fresh and new. We can all be creative in the same ways, by taking something we know in one area or domain of life and bringing it to another that seems completely unrelated.

Bob Benkowski loved space and the unknown. He had a fascination with flying in space and loved getting off the ground – in fact, he was able to fly an airplane before he could drive a car. Later he would learn he had a unique ability to see the overlap in medicine and space. It was that ability to see the connections that allowed him to create various new products, many of which he and his team have healthcare patents on today.

Before his healthcare career, Benkowski started working on the B1 bomber and then the C17 as an aeronautical engineer. He worked at Johnson Space Center on the Space Station at the beginning of the program, eventually moving from airplanes to aerospace. Fairly early in his career there, the organization needed a volunteer to help with the computer modeling for the development of an implantable blood pump. Benkowski made some computer models and helped make prototypes, and that's how he made the switch from aerospace to computers through his computer modeling, which was his specialty. He had grounded knowledge they needed and was in the right place at the right time.

Benkowski has a unique perspective on how medicine and space overlap – it's everywhere, he tells me. Oil fields and medicine also have overlaps. He explained that when you look at fluid fuel – the blood in our veins and the fluids in a space shuttle – there's a lot of crossover between them. When you find the overlap between fields, you can leverage expertise, and that opens up a whole new world of possibilities. Consider how pumping rocket fuel overlaps with pumping blood. That's the overlap Benkowski was looking at. NASA had spent a full third of its budget to learn how people fare in space – it was heavily invested in this critical understanding. NASA was interested in how space affected astronauts and bodies and how people can perform in space. Benkowski would later pour himself into electro-mechanical devices and implantable hearts in the biomedical field, informed from his experience working in pumping fuels into rockets.

I heartily suggest you do this exercise with your team. Assemble them in a room all facing each other and focus the conversation on a problem or opportunity in your area that you need to address. Ask each person on the team to consider how that problem would have manifested, been solved, or addressed in their previous company – especially if they worked in a different industry. Listen with curiosity to what is offered and be open to the fresh insights or reinforcing links that emerge. Celebrate the discussion and be sure to acknowledge and thank everyone for their input. They will appreciate feeling heard and contributing their previously gained experience.

Life is 'Awe'-some – Don't Miss It!

By now I hope I've convinced you to look more deeply for inspiration and to allow it to work its power across your life and certainly your leadership. Now, let's take it one step further beyond curiosity and creativity, and layer in another distinction: the transportive emotion of awe. Being in awe means living and leaning into the powerful feeling of reverence, admiration, power, and respect for the world around us. I like author Emily Esfahani Smith's description of this emotion in her book, *The Power of Meaning: Crafting a Life That Matters.*[53] She refers to it as a sense of wonder felt in the

---

[53] E. Esfahani-Smith, *The Power of Meaning: Crafting a Life That Matters,* 2017.

presence of something vast that surpasses our understanding of the world. Awe is one of the few human emotions that stops time while you experience it and grounds you in the present. In awe, humans transcend their everyday place in the world and rise above it to experience a higher reality, communing with a more sacred world. Esfahani Smith shares that when you experience awe, you actually challenge your mental models to make sense of the world. Thus, your mind must then update those models to accommodate what you have just experienced. To experience awe is to engage with life in a way that elevates your consciousness and being to a higher level.

Awe, like any of our emotions, is evoked in each person differently. For some, a feeling of awe comes from profound experiences with the mystical and sacred. Music or art can evoke it for some. For others, like me, it can come from everyday encounters with nature. Regardless of its origin, experiencing awe has many benefits. It has been linked to enhanced critical and creative thinking competencies, perhaps precisely because of how it elevates the mental models to process the emotion and according experience. Experiencing awe is linked to reduced levels of stress, which translate to improved health in today's fast-paced living. Experiencing awe, and reflecting on it, opens a sense of interconnectedness to something bigger. In other words, it's as if one can see the otherwise previously invisible threads that connect seemingly disparate entities across space and time. Finally, the experience of awe has been linked to increases in pro-social behaviors such as kindness, self-sacrifice, cooperation, and resource sharing. Awe opens our hearts, elevates us to a higher plane, and fuels our energy tanks.

As I open myself to increasing experiences with awe, I develop greater access to its power – and of course I want the same for you. To assist in your access to awe, let me share two recent experiences with nature that qualify as awe-inspiring or awe-inducing. One spring evening in 2019, I arrived back to my home at about 8.00 pm. I parked my car in my driveway under the tree and was stepping out of it to my front door of my home when immediately over my head, I heard a 'hooo hooo' directed squarely in my direction. I felt picked up out of my body – almost as if I didn't have one in that instant. I immediately replied, raising my head to gaze up into the dark tree above, attempting to mirror the creature's same marvelous sound with a corresponding 'hooo hooo.'

Now realizing I was conversing with him, the owl replied, and the two of us volleyed back and forth several times until I finally 'came to.' I remembered my teenage daughter was inside the house and I simply had to share this experience with her. I ran from the driveway to the front door, opened it, and called for her to come outside. By this time, my new friend the owl had hopped over from the tree above the driveway where our initial exchange had taken place to the tree outside my front door – as if he wanted more of the conversation and didn't want to let it go. When my daughter came to the door, I turned over my shoulder and called out, 'hoo hooo,' and my owl returned a response one last time and then fell silent. I stood feeling as though I'd been specially selected by nature and the universe, grateful beyond measure, and most certainly transported to a higher level.

I'm happy to report that the experience I had is duplicatable. I shared this owl-friend encounter with participants enrolled in the Vitally Inspired – Living with Passion and Leading from Purpose program not long after the event occurred. It's quite likely that at least a few of them thought I was a crackpot and more than a little 'out there' as they listened to the story. About three weeks later, one of the participants who'd heard the story sent me a text on a Sunday at 11.34 pm. It read:

ALISE!!!! I JUST TALKED TO AN OWL!! Seriously! I saw him perched on a wire as I was walking my dog. It was dark but I could tell by the shape of his head. So I

hooted two times and he hooted back!! We did this four or five times. It was AWESOME!! Emphasis on the AWE!!!
(Vitally Inspired program participant, May 2019)

Awe and its enlarging contribution don't just come from experiencing nature, as I just shared. Awe can also come through the experience of hearing achingly beautiful music or seeing a human doing the impossible (like the witness reports of a mother lifting a car to free a trapped child). It can certainly come from bearing witness to profoundly spiritual or religious encounters that evoke the unforgettable emotion of awe that leaves a person transported. To experience awe on a regular basis, you will need to cultivate an openness to experience and employ a childlike enjoyment of the moment. You will be amazed at just how good it feels to 'be a kid again' and revel in the moment. Let your guard down and open yourself up to the world. Encourage your team to do the same and watch how camaraderie and innovation escalate off the charts.

Final Thoughts on Inspiration

Cultivating inspiration in your life is a lot like anything else – it takes practice and ongoing commitment. It takes allowing yourself to be vulnerable and tender to the touch, to let the world in and to wash over you and unleash you from self-limitations of who you should be and how you should act. When you allow yourself to stand in the realm of possibilities and gaze at what 'could be,' rather than limit yourself in what you're sure is simply 'not possible' today, a whole new vista opens up. It lifts you, holds you gently up above the earth, letting you gaze at that which had formerly been 'below.' What if peace actually *were* possible? What if every child got to go to bed at night with a belly full of food and fall asleep in a warm bed? What if your team really could launch that product three months faster? What if you could create that income stream for your business you've been wondering about? What if ...?

To fully register and enjoy the effects of inspiration requires an openness to experience, allowing a certain vulnerability. With it comes moments of inconvenience, by which I mean allowing yourself to be picked up and carried away by what life pours into you. That emotion can be overwhelming for those newly initiated. Take heart – it will get easier. Letting other people see you take in the world and be bowled over by it is a lot like being naked in front of a crowd. But soon you will get used to the idea that yours is just a body and disregard how others will judge it, and instead melt into the experience of the moment. No stiff upper lip. No girding against the swelling emotion. Just let it pour into you and infuse you with essential, life-giving energy. When you find yourself so moved by the goodness life serves up, the opportunity is to truly *let* yourself fall into the moment, collapse into the feeling. Doing so will likely evoke tears. Who cares? At the end of your life, do you want to be able to say, 'I steeled myself strong in life and let nothing creep into my soul?' Or do you want to be able to say, 'I've *tasted* life, savored every moment. It was precious, glorious. And completely delicious. And I've devoured a beautiful life'? I know what I would choose. So, lean in, let the world and its glorious array of experiences breathe life into you. Don't turn this critical first aid away.

As you lean into and become more open to inspiration, you will start to notice that this openness gives you fresh eyes to enjoy the mystery of the world around you and thread together seemingly disparate phenomena. And that, my friend, goes hand in hand with the wonder of curiosity. You can freely play, express, and see myriad delightful connections that previously eluded you. As you sharpen your ability to be more fully present with the world and let its enchantment wash over you, a natural by-product is that you'll be more open and able to experiencing the wonder of awe, a refined emotion that transports you to a higher plane and changes the mental models with which you make sense of life. Whereas at a lower vibrational and developmental level, you might have 'missed' the moment, having cultivated your inspirational capacity, you can 'catch' those glorious moments and let them fill your tank with wonder and energy that lights your life and steels your resolve. From that life-affirming and enriching stance, you are so fortified by what the world infuses into you that your energy and person are positively irresistible to those you encounter. You literally radiate vitality, goodness, and grace. That is the power of being inspired. Let it infuse you with energy and open you to greater possibilities and wonders of the world. It's worth the journey and the laid-bare openness its effectiveness requires. You can do it – especially when working from your purpose, which we'll discuss next.

Key Points and Exercises

Seek Out Inspiration
For at least a week, go looking each day for at least one thing that inspires you. Record the instance/experience in your journal and include the before and after effect of how you felt and how experiencing this inspiration changed your energy and outlook. Make sure at least one of those experiences happens at work.

Honor Yourself
Where across your life are you not honoring who you really know yourself to be – whether that means you're also an artist when the rest of the world knows you to be a super savvy investor or business leader, or deep down you're someone who cares radically about the environment and abhors the pollution we contribute to it and stand for doing something about it? What's stopping you from advancing that initiative at work you care so much about? Consider, deep down, who you're hiding from the outside world? Why? What are you afraid of? By modeling your own vulnerability, how can you help your team members step out to claim more of their own authenticity?

Elevate Yourself
Read the newspaper or do an online search and summon one or two possibilities that would inspire you and elevate you above where you are today. These possibilities could include finally having a close, connected, and respectful relationship with your teenager or significant other, starting a non-profit foundation that serves your community in a way that matters to you or someone you love, or helping to take the start-up company you helped found to IPO. Are any of those areas something that is

connected to a grander meaning in your life – even your own purpose?

Live Authentically

Download the Inauthenticity Cost matrix from www.alisecortez.com or www.gusto-now.com – it will guide you to write a list of two columns.

On the left, where are you being inauthentic in your life? What's the area? Why do you think you are doing this? What is it costing you? On the right, where are you practicing and living authentically? Why are you able to do so in that part of your life? What's present or helping to make it possible? How does that authenticity pay off for you? How can you fold more of that authentic effort into the other parts of your life to bring them to fruition and authenticity?

Seek Out Inspiration

Add a daily reminder to your calendar on Sunday or Monday morning to start the week fresh, to go looking for experiences and interactions that move you, both at work and beyond it. Get yourself into a mental, emotional, and spiritual place to let yourself be moved by the world around you. Let the experiences wash over you. Record the interactions and how you are moved in your journal. Begin to notice how these experiences elevate you to living on a higher vibration of energy and consciousness. Notice how your own interactions begin to be informed by, and change and grow due to, these experiences being folded into you.

Surprise Yourself with Creativity

Take a look at two completely different aspects of your life (maybe whatever your professional life is and a hobby of yours – say, cooking.) Look for how those two areas have similarities or could inform or improve the way something is done in the other. Write down your findings. Now, look for three ways you could take something pertinent from one field and bring it into the other to create some new look, mode of operation, or even new product or service.

Discover Awe

Take an 'awe walk,' which involves going somewhere that has the potential to evoke awe in you. This could be your own familiar surroundings, the area you live in, your backyard, the park near your home, or a stroll down your own street. Consider the simple joy of a child laughing as a potential area to seek awe. As you observe your surroundings, look at them through fresh eyes, as if you've been going through life blindfolded, taking in what you see as if for the very first time. When you are present and paying attention, something as simple as a shock of red quickly passing in front of you, disguised as a cardinal bird, might just take your breath away and change the way you go about the rest of your day.

Video: *Inspiration: Seeking Constant Breath in Life*

Watch this video at www.alisecortez.com or www.gusto-now.com

What are three new ideas you got while viewing that can be applied to your own life and leadership?

6

Purpose: Your Reason for Being That Makes the World a Better Place

You started the journey in the first chapter of this book by discussing meaning, in depth. Now, after learning more about identity, wellbeing, passion, and inspiration, it is time to turn the focus to purpose. Let me clarify that what is meant by purpose in this book is quite personal (for the individual) and specific (for the company). Here's what I don't mean – 'breakfast on purpose' or 'I do my life, on purpose.' These slogans refer to a certain intentionality. That's not what this chapter is about. Rather, the meaning of purpose, discussed more in detail in subsequent segments, is closer to your *raison d'être*, or your reason for being – your 'why'.

If I had a nickel for each person I've encountered over the last 10 years who has expressed to me, 'I just wish I knew what I was supposed to be doing with my life,' I think I could easily have amassed a small fortune. People are hungry to discover and live their purpose. Much has been written about how to find one's purpose, including magical moments in childhood, challenging or crucible experiences that happen at any point in life, or activities that excite us over long periods of time (Nick Craig).[54] Others distinguish that purpose must involve serving a group bigger than yourself, call forth your own personal growth, and involve building a community (Aaron Hurst).[55] No matter how you get there, each person's path is distinctively their own. Purpose is not so much a destination, but rather a path.

Whatever route you take to get there, discovering your purpose is electrifying. It gives you a spectacular motivation and crazy energy to go after your dreams and persevere through the inevitable and often innumerable challenges. Discovering and living from your purpose makes you irresistible to others, who often feel drawn to you and desperately want to be involved in whatever cause or project you're up to. I have witnessed this phenomenon personally over and over again while out speaking on the very topics you're reading about in this book, only to be approached by audience members who excitedly proclaim how they want to join my team and be part of whatever it is I'm up to! It's beautiful and it humbles me every time.

Here's the caveat: discovering and living your purpose usually does take some serious, concerted effort. Pursuing your purpose is a choice and a journey that unfolds over time. It's not a luxury reserved just for citizens of well-capitalized countries but rather a direction to pursue for us all. Purpose is available to anyone and in any kind of work. It may not always be convenient to discover and live your purpose, but doing so has so many other counterbalancing positives, which you'll learn about in the sections that follow in this chapter. Purpose takes courage. It takes – and gives – a tremendous amount of energy. The return on your investment is like nothing you've ever seen before.

---

[54] N. Craig, *Leading from Purpose: Clarity and Confidence When it Matters Most*, 2018.

[55] A. Hurst, *The Purpose Economy: How Your Desire for Impact, Personal Growth, and Community is Changing the World*, 2019.

In this chapter, you'll learn to look for your purpose through an even deeper gaze into what makes you unique and learn some ways to discover your purpose if you don't know it already. You'll recognize the role a finite life has to power purpose and how a well-crafted eulogy can keep you on point to pursue it. As time marches on across your lifespan, you'll learn why you may be registering a greater sense of urgency to pursue your purpose in your forties and fifties.

Uniquely You

Have you ever considered just what it took for you to be created? The sheer number of forces that conspired in the world – all to usher in *you?* The odds of your parents meeting in the first place? That you came into the world at the exact time, place, and country you did? And consider the lineage that brought you forth, the generations who opened the way before you. What you look like and the unique qualities that make you who you are: magnificent. Then there's conception. I once heard a priest share the perspective on just how unique each of us is by the profundity that hundreds of thousands or even millions of sperm that competed against one another to fertilize one singular egg – and just one of those sperm won the race to meet the egg and create *you*. Now, that's something special and unique. And that something is you.

Consider just one area of your person that is exquisitely unique and recognizable by people all over the world: your face. Want a fun example? Now, I do understand we must factor in fame here, but I have to share that I had the wonderful experience of encountering, and immediately recognizing one Dr Ruth Westheimer (the famous sex therapist known as 'Dr Ruth')[56] in a hotel in Jerusalem, Israel in January 1993. I'll

---

[56] To learn more about Dr Ruth, visit https://en.wikipedia.org/wiki/Ruth_Westheimer

confess: I did know her face immediately – what shocked me was her short stature, nylon stockings, and platform shoes. I really did not associate those accessories with a sex therapist! But I did know immediately who they adorned. What I did not know at the time is that Dr Ruth is Jewish and has close ties to Israel, and has spent a fair amount of time there – hence, it would have been much more natural for her to be in Israel than I ever imagined. Nonetheless, I immediately recognized her by her face. And I had traveled from Rio de Janeiro, Brazil (where I lived at the time), as an American, to be there. It was a colossal juxtaposition of many forces colliding that nonetheless presented a singular person in a moment of time I immediately recognized as unique among us – among anyone walking the planet.

As your uniquely created person, no matter what your face looks like or who can recognize it, you will spend your life cultivating yourself as you move with your own beat across time, and see your life's wonder and opportunity through your own special lens. No one else can quite do *you* the way you can. Your job in life is to discover how this specially crafted being that is you is purposed to exist. Prepare for a lifetime of adventure in this pursuit – the better acquainted you are with you and your purpose, the more you have to draw from to make the contribution worthy of your life.

Whether you're yet aware of your purpose, it is acting as a unique filter through which you see the world, as discussed in Chapter 1. Looking through that specific and unique lens, each of us sees possibilities or does something that others would not have seen or done. That difference is the source of innovation and impact to which we all aspire. Your purpose can never be taken from you – it's who you are at your core.

I acquired a deeper understanding of the distinction of uniqueness and how it manifests through purpose lived in a conversation with Marty Ruiz.[57] I invited Marty to share his

---

[57] *Working on Purpose* episode 2, Voice America, 2/11/2015.

story on *Working on Purpose* – he was my second guest ever. Marty discovered his purpose to bring delight to and connect elderly people living in their retirement homes back to the same genres of music they loved in their youth and early adulthood (the 1950s) – the very music he loves to sing. He is completely in his element, grateful to be serving a need, and fully booked for months! The music he loves and can sing well allows him the opportunity to perform in retirement homes during the day so he can be at home with the one he loves at night (understand how unusual this scenario might be for other artists or musicians, who often spend their time playing music all night and into the early morning hours at clubs and bars, often at the detriment of connection to significant others with a very different schedule).

Marty's story is noteworthy in how it unfolded to show him his own unique ability to do what he does in his career and appreciate how fulfilling his life is because of it. He had always known that he was born an artist. Over a lifetime, he would work in the jewelry business, render canvas paintings, and create greeting cards. Later he was producing paintings that he knew were distinguished and that people appreciated, yet that work didn't seem to register as having the impact on the community that he was seeking. He wondered how to elevate himself to living his purpose with those artistic innate talents and make the difference to which he aspired. He managed to do just that – he turned his volunteer hobby of singing for free at retirement homes and villages into a paid, fulfilling vocation that allows him a comfortable work–life harmony and he couldn't be happier about how special his talents are and his joy in their unique service to the world that affords his living.

Marty shared the delight he experiences when out singing to people in retirement homes, many of whom are beginning to lose their memories. As he sings the songs that remind them of their early productive years working and raising children, people otherwise battling dementia often raise their hands to their faces, tears streaming down their faces, as they suddenly recall where they were when they heard that very song. In other words, not only does Marty's song entertain and delight the audience, it brings back memories that otherwise had drifted away to some distant recess of their mind. Music has incredible healing and connecting power. And Marty's intimate knowledge of his purpose and according expressive talent of song heals and entertains his audiences while fueling his soul. What a wonderful way to celebrate his own uniqueness and *work on purpose*.

Discovering Your Purpose

By now you may be wondering, with all this talk about purpose interwoven in the preceding chapters, what *is* it, exactly? What counts for purpose? Authors have defined the term in various ways, with William Damon describing purpose as 'the forward-pointing arrow that motivates our behavior and serves as the organizing principle for our lives.'[58] I think this definition aligns well with my own conceptualization of the term. Then there is Zach Mercurio's[59] definition of purpose, which is 'the reason for your unique existence that betters the world.'[60] That definition expands the previous one. Aaron Hurst's[61] perspective on the term offers three criteria for what people are up to in life that together comprise purpose, with which I also align: the activity must be in service of a group of people bigger than yourself; you will be stretched and personally grow in the service of your purpose; and you will

[58] W. Damon, *The Path to Purpose: How Young People Find Their Calling in Life*, 2009.

[59] *Working on Purpose* episode 183, Voice America, 8/8/2018.

[60] Z. Mercurio, *The Invisible Leader: Transform Your Life, Work and Organization with the Power of Authentic Purpose*, 2017.

[61] *Working on Purpose* episode 191, Voice America, 10/3/2018.

build a community in service of your purpose. To combine those perspectives, I offer that your purpose is that which you pursue in service to others that uniquely expresses what your special lens allows you to see in the world.

People across the globe are hungry to discover their purpose. When more of us do, there will naturally be less talk about it as an overt word – its agentic power will become more of the natural order of how life is expected to be. It is only because it seems to elude so many people that we place such an inordinate focus on it. I am convinced that purpose will soon be 'baked in' to normal, everyday life, becoming the standard. And it will happen because children and young people will gain access to it in their youth and not in mid-life when things seem to be otherwise incomplete for them.

Until that day comes, there are some ways to gain greater access to your own purpose as you navigate reading this book and go forward in life and work. A first place to look is at what has ailed you for most or all of your life? What desperate question have you been trying to answer or what dilemma have you been trying to solve for yourself? Is it the question, 'Why can't I stop obsessing about my weaknesses – and focus instead on my strengths and use them as an anchor to advance my career?' Or is it, 'Why do I struggle to focus and learn new things?' My preoccupation for decades was how I could realize the best version of myself and really *do* something with myself, which as a purpose statement today becomes 'I exist to awaken people to their passion and purpose and inspire them to contribute them mightily to make a contribution worthy of their one, precious life.'

Another way to look for your purpose is by considering what major force life event(s) – or 'crucible moments,' as author Nick Craig[62] calls them – you have navigated to help you become who you are today, Look for what was in those events, situation, or circumstance that called something in

---

[62] *Working on Purpose* episode 210, Voice America, 2/13/2019.

you to respond; the way you did so *made* you into who you are today. For some, it's surviving cancer and becoming an advocate for self-care to avoid others getting this disease in the first place, which is a way to characterize Gwen Rich's journey to purpose (which you learned about earlier in the book).[63] For others, it's rising inside an organization as a leader against all odds and pulling the team through to a tremendous victory, all the while second-guessing their own competencies and secretly worrying that they're imposters and don't deserve to be in the role.

Passion is another place to look. What completely consumes your attention? What activity, topic, or cause do you continually turn to and can't put down – a focus area that has persisted for years? If you follow your curiosity and what really lights you up or what you pour yourself into, you just might find a bucket of purpose at the bottom of the barrel. In my case, I *love* empowering and emboldening people. That's a big part of how I do the work I do today – it's the package in which any of my services come. I know that for people to make their biggest, best contribution in expression of their purpose, they will need to be emboldened and have to push well beyond obstacles and limitations.

Finally, another place to look for purpose is to consider what big, wicked or hairy problem you stand for solving or addressing in the world. Is it that your community just does not seem to get out and vote and you want more citizens to get on board and participate in a democratic society? Maybe you will become a spokesperson for this initiative – or run for office yourself. Is your area of your community considered a 'food desert,' where there are no sources of real food or wholesome groceries, but rather just an occasional convenience store with processed or fast food? Perhaps your purpose is to start or join an organization, or a division or initiative inside your company, that addresses that lack through food distribution

---

[63] *Working on Purpose* episode 186, Voice America, 8/29/2018.

or some other approach to providing healthy whole food or access to it to the community.

As you turn over the above questions in your mind and a focus area starts to appear, consider the basic questions taught in journalism: who, when, where, what, how, and why. Who do you want to help – what kinds of people or organizations or entities? I exist to serve leaders inside organizations who want to be part of the solution, treating the existential vacuum and creating cultures of meaning, and inspiring people to discover and work from their purpose, being fulfilled in life and at work. I continue working with individuals who are hungry for more – more meaning, more fulfillment, more purpose – to help them work toward realizing what they can become in their one, precious life.

The 'when' question for me is when the company is not achieving the business results it wants and a more motivated, aligned, and innovative workforce could help win the day. 'Where' is, wonderfully, all over the world as I travel physically or virtually to companies to consult and facilitate programs; they are available online in the *Catch Fire* and *Gusto Now* communities to individuals and inside organizations, and via the speaking I do at conferences and in my weekly radio show. 'What' takes the form of the programs I created and offer to empower and enliven people to lives of passion, inspiration, meaning, and purpose. That 'what' will always be informed with my particular 'how' brand of empowerment and inspiration. My 'why?' Because living my purpose is the best version of life I have encountered so far. It is incredibly energizing, enlivening, and fulfilling, and I've never lived on this kind of level so sustainably and vitally since discovering and living my purpose. And because the world desperately needs as many of us as possible living on the planet living with passion and working on purpose to take on the plethora of problems and opportunities that exist.

There are countless stories from the radio program I could share about people finding and living their purpose. Brittany

Merrill, founder and CEO of the Akola Project,[64] realized she had a passion and calling in her work while a student on a break from college. On a trip to Uganda, she saw poverty worse than she'd ever witnessed. She met a Ugandan woman in the community who lived in a shack and saw how this woman was living with incredible meaning and purpose, sacrificing everything to feed and care for three children in her home, often going without food herself. This experience greatly impacted Brittany, and she reflected on how much she'd been given in life but felt she hadn't done enough in return. The bewildering 'aha moment' shook her out of complacency and ignited a fire in her heart and soul.

Brittany graduated from Southern Methodist University in 2006 and moved to Uganda to build an orphanage project there. She started Akola (which means 'she works') while there, explaining that it solved the same problems addressed by orphanages but in a different way. Brittany and her organizational team quickly learned that if they could work through women to keep the kids in their homes with them by creating income-generating opportunities to provide a living wage with holistic empowerment opportunities, it was possible to ignite meaningful change in these communities that could help bring children out of poverty. Brittany has been doing this work since age 19 and was 33 at the time of the interview.

Brittany spent the majority of her twenties living in East African villages and contracted many types of sicknesses. Sometimes she didn't have running water or electricity. She exclaimed how these experiences had taught her so much. People around her questioned what she was doing, and she realized it was her passion and calling. She discovered her passion while committing to something really hard, right, true, and in service to others. This is the power of purpose!

Today, the Akola Project[65] is a globally inspired brand that creates striking jewelry designed to lift up, nourish, and

---

[64] *Working on Purpose* episode 141, Voice America, 10/11/2017.
[65] To learn more about Akola, visit https://akola.co.

champion women around the world. The organization also provides life-changing job opportunities through vertically integrated manufacturing, employing nearly 200 women in Uganda to make each piece of jewelry. Brittany is a reminder that there's so much inside each of us that can change the world and encourages us to dive in and not be afraid, stay committed, and persevere. Amazing things can happen when we do.

Death – Yours

There's something anti-social, ghastly, really almost taboo when death is raised as a subject of discussion, especially if it's your own. Most people don't want to think about this guaranteed rite of passage, as it conjures at least unpleasant thoughts if not outright angst and panic. But there is an undeniable truth that everyone will all one day cease to exist: this singular, unescapable reality of life is an inordinately important catalyst that drives purpose. Without this unavoidable hard stop, it would be easy to coast complacently through an unending life 'with all the time in the world,' never really optimizing the experience. Consider that your death is a fundamental *part of your life,* as its sure approach helps frame intention and gives a sense of urgency to achieve, impact, or seek to be remembered. Death catalyzes purpose.

Until recently, I'd had little experience with death. Then both of my parents passed away in January 2019. Losing my mother, and the father who adopted me at age 8, was a surreal experience. My mother was completely ready to end her life of suffering with chronic obstructive pulmonary disease (COPD). When she passed in the early morning hours of January 3, 2019 at age 73, I was lying next to her in her single hospital bed. She was here one moment, and quite literally gone the next. There was something so sobering about that momentary passing that I still can't quite absorb or fully comprehend. But it has further instilled in me and surfaces in my own messaging while speaking and conducting programs the tremendous gift we have in living each and every day to the fullest and with gratitude. When my Dad followed my mom just 28 days later, while in good health at age 78, I had no choice but to fully confront the size and force of my contender death, knowing that one day I'd forfeit the match too. Confronting this reality square on has fortified me in a race against time and fueled my fire to do and be everything I so desperately want to make of myself and give to the world while I'm here. I hope with all of my being that reading this book is helping to do the same for you.

I almost missed the amazing good fortune to connect with a *perfect* person to help me deepen my understanding of the role of death in living and working on purpose. The opportunity knock came from Elizabeth Fournier,[66] who is affectionally called 'the green reaper' for her earth-friendly burial advocacy. She had reached out to me to request being a guest on the *Working on Purpose* radio program. I read her inquiry many times over the course of a few months and kept saying to myself, 'What is she *thinking*?! Why does an undertaker want to be on my show?' And I further mused, 'I'm about passion, inspiration, and purpose – I don't *do* death. Nope, this is not a guest for me.' And then finally, thank goodness, I got the 'aha' moment I needed: I made the connection that she was the *most qualified* person I'd encountered to talk about how our certain death *fuels* purpose!

With that sudden realization, I immediately dialed the number she listed on the inquiry email. She was surprised to hear from me, as she'd emailed me several months prior. I told her about my 'aha' moment and invited her to come on the show to talk from that vantage point. Elizabeth is the owner/operator of Cornerstone Funeral Services in Oregon

---

[66] *Working on Purpose* episode 199, Voice America, 11/28/2018.

and is the zestiest undertaker I've ever met. What a delight! Death is her business and I learned in the course of the conversation that it's also her calling, which is why she had initially reached out to be a guest on the show in the first place. She knew she was working on purpose. Her mother died when she was only eight years old. She went to countless funerals as a 'crasher' to try to understand death and life, until age thirteen when she came to understand that this was the profession where she belonged. She even lived on a cemetery grounds for four years while in college.

It was Elizabeth who helped me understand that death is simply part of the cycle of life. She sees her work as primarily serving the living – those left behind by the departed. Elizabeth has a unique vantage point on life and purpose precisely because she has helped so many people to close the final chapter of their lives. She'd heard many people and those they left behind express regret for things they did not say or do prior to the final curtain coming down. The best-lived lives, though, were recounted by people who navigated a life with a complete sense of gratitude, another essential ingredient in living with passion and working on purpose, discussed in Chapter 3. The lesson here is to become present to the idea that your life is finite – and you are well served to make the most of it, directed from your purpose.

At Your Funeral: The Eulogy

While we're on the topic of death, we might as well discuss funerals – yours, specifically. Have you ever considered just what the event commemorating your death – really, your life – might be like? Writing your own eulogy for the person you aspire to become is one of the exercises completed by participants in my *Vitally Inspired – Living and Leading from Purpose* programs – and it's one I highly recommend for you as well. Before you write your eulogy, list the sum total of your life that you would most want for yourself. What would you most desire of your life? Who did you become? What contributions did you make to the people closest to you, your community, work, society at large? Who were you as a leader? What adventures did you pour yourself into? What great love did you give and receive? Remember, this is the person you ardently aspire to become, not necessarily the person you are today.

Now, consider that final commemoration of your life – your funeral, or however you will be put to rest. What are people saying about you in your eulogy – what was your contribution to their lives? What will they miss about you? Going through this work/exercise can be a very sobering and incredibly directing exercise. You might even want to try a practice run at this. Consider that my dear Roland (my early boss) asked me to help him plan his 80th birthday party in 2016, which would take the form of a 'living wake.' He said, 'I don't want to have to be dead to hear what people have to say about me! I'd like that feedback *now*!' Think about it. Depending on what people in attendance say about you, you may need a serious course correction to finish things the way you like!

Set your intention to be someone you're proud of – always, no matter who sees or doesn't. You will spend a lot of your life in your own company, snuggled up with your own thoughts as you do laundry, drive to and from work, pick up the kids, and grocery shop. Those moments that seem 'in between the rest of life' are actually threads of your overall existence. Who you are in those fleeting moments is an important part of your life story. Do you warmly greet the person on the street corner asking for money or help outside the post office or grocery store? Or do you scoff at them? Are you patient with the older person who seems to be taking an eternity to back out of that parking spot? Do you hit the horn? Or imagine your own parents – yourself – there some day and be more compassionate? Do you offer to help guide them out of their parking spot? Who do you desperately want to be? Identity drives behavior, choices, and action, as discussed in Chapter 2. Decide... Be judicious. Your life, its contents, and your legacy literally depend on it. You will enjoy the eulogy given on your behalf so much more if you do.

I'm certain countless other people who've lost their parents also received the gift of a driving sense of directed purpose. Maybe you're one of them? Rabbi Daniel Cohen[67] lost his beloved mother when he was 21. Her passing instilled in him an acute awareness of the fragility of life and the gift of every day. This life-altering event heightened his sense of urgency to realize his own potential and to do his utmost every day to harness all his energy and talents to help other people realize their own potential.

Rabbi Cohen and I talked about his book, *What Will They Say About You When You are Gone?*,[68] in which he describes the importance of reverse-engineering your life and provides seven principles for doing so. He orients the reader to the importance of eulogy and reverse-engineering our lives with this snippet:

> *Throughout the history of humanity, humans have striven to become immortal ... we strive to outlast our mortality and defeat death. This isn't because we know we can physically transcend the limits of time but because programmed into our DNA is a desire to be remembered, to lead a life of significance. We all want to know we have made some everlasting contribution to this world.*[69]

Beginning with the desired end in mind in this way opens a space to let go of the worries and confines of today and enter

---

[67] *Working on Purpose* episode 222, Voice America, 5/8/2019.

[68] D. Cohen, *What Will They Say About You When You're Gone? Creating a Life of Legacy*, 2016.

[69] Cohen, *What Will They Say About You?*, p. 118.

a mystical world of the decidedly unknown and possible. I dare say it's a place of creativity and dreams – as well it should be, given you're about to architect your one, precious life. Be bold! Be audacious! Who are you not to be? Create this bold vision of your eulogy and end and keep it present, so the future literally pulls you into it. Keeping that vision firmly in mind helps guide your choices, how you spend your time and treat people, and what you do with all your resources. Begin with the end in mind – and be sure to delight in the ending of your story.

Half-time as the Game Starter

There's another important accelerator in this whole business of purpose, and that's the idea of 'half-time.' For this, I must thank author Dan Pink for alerting me to the idea and how it can provide a powerful sense of urgency and fortify effort. In Pink's book, *When: The Scientific Secrets of Perfect Timing,*[70] he talks about studies he and others have done to analyze football and basketball games. He writes that teams that find themselves slightly behind at half-time often go on to win the game. He attributes this phenomenon to the motivation that can be summoned when a turnaround to win from behind seems very challenging – but still within grasp. In other words, the 'half-time' phenomenon fortifies purpose – and gives it urgency.

Until I read these words, and heard him speak at a conference on the topic, I had not been able to determine why in my early fifties my focus to realize my goals, dreams, and purpose was so pressing. I was 52 years old and had been feeling decidedly behind at the half-time of my life. In my case, I didn't feel *slightly* behind – I felt *woefully* behind in realizing the vision I had for my life. The fire lit by this

---

[70] D. Pink, *When: The Scientific Secrets of Perfect Timing,* 2018.

half-time phenomenon, especially when Dan Pink helped bring it to my consciousness in his book and at the conference, has been enormously energizing and has helped focus my energies on creating the life I want for myself. People – get out of my way, I'm comin' through! I've got stuff to do and the clock is ticking!

Over the course of pursuing a PhD in human development, I drank deeply of the lifespan psychology authors who study people across the whole of their lives. Gail Sheehy describes in similar terms in her book *Passages: Predictable Crises of Adult Life*[71] what Pink calls this 'half-time' phenomenon. She describes midlife as being accompanied by a certain shift in psychic energies toward the inner self and a directed focus to give life greater meaning while becoming more aware of mortality to create a renewed purpose. If you are in your forties or fifties, there's a good chance that you've experienced this insistent nudging. The opportunity is to be still enough to hear it, and to let it inform and govern you to create the life you desire for yourself so you can fully live your purpose.

There are many examples on which I could draw to illustrate this idea of 'half-time' and the intense dose of motivation it provides to run after our dreams. Here, I'll introduce you to James 'Jay' Archer.[72] After many successful ventures in his career, Jay finally found his true calling at age 52. He'd had a strong inkling early in his life that languages and the humanities were the direction he should take for his career, but the conservative times in which he was reared dictated the practical, tried and true field of engineering. He enjoyed a long career and much success in this technical field and others, only to discover that after a half-century of life, this insistent inner calling could no longer be silenced. It only took a six-week immersion trip to Costa Rica where

---

[71] G. Sheehy, *Passages: Predictable Crises of Adult Life*, 2006.

[72] *Working on Purpose* episode 36, Voice America, 10/7/2015.

Spanish was the only medium of communication to ignite the flame. Jay shared with me how this experience and his love of language resulted in the ShareLingo Project, a social enterprise that aims to make a lasting difference to the world by connecting cultures, breaking down stereotypes that separate people from different backgrounds and social levels, and better unifying the people of the planet.[73] Jay knew he wanted to work until he died – he just didn't want to work for somebody else. When he founded the ShareLingo Project, he knew it was his life's purpose – very compelling to run after in the middle part of life.

In our subsequent conversations and ongoing connection, Jay and I have talked about both our respective manifestations of the 'half-time' phenomenon. He has told me that he deeply wants to leave a legacy for his children to remember him by while serving the world in his mission. His commitment and dedication to the ShareLingo Project are governed by an intense work ethic to keep developing the platform and bring more people the gift of learning a second language with native speakers. He's passionate about bringing cultures together and uniting people across the world in meaningful dialogue and connection. That desired end-game is his purpose, fueled intensely by 'half-time' motivation, which intensely governs his work ethic and commitment. What's haunting *you?* What do you feel compelled toward? What do you *need* to address, put yourself into solving? Pay very close attention to this inner summons: it is desperately trying to tell you where to direct your purpose.

Final Thoughts on Purpose

Purpose is a powerful force in today's world. Purpose – your purpose specifically – is the most tender and dynamic aspect

---

[73] Visit www.sharelingo.org for more information.

that makes you *you*. It is the unique and rare reason for your existence, and when applied, makes the world a better place. In the service of your purpose, you will be amazed at the crazy energy, courage, and creativity that accompany it.

While it can be uncomfortable to consider, the surety of your own morality and ultimate death can actually channel and fortify your purpose. Why? Precisely because knowing you have an unknown, finite number of days fuels an intensity to live each day to its fullest, and helps you resist the urge to numb away discomfort as you grow into your purpose and bring everything you've got to its pursuit. Death is a gift in in life that helps ensure that you stay focused and constantly nurture your passion, inspiration, and purpose. Without it, apathy in what would seem a utopian society could actually be the ultimate demise as motivation would likely be entirely eradicated as people floated effortlessly forever.

Adding more fuel to the fire, there is something about coming to 'half-time' in your forties and fifties that is often associated with a renewed vigor and motivation to pursue meaning and purpose as you start to recognize your looming mortality. You can channel this urgent feeling to fuel your goals, passion, and purpose toward an effective aim. A way to ignite that motivational flame even more strongly is to write the eulogy you most want delivered when you've passed. Standing in that distant, future state, away from all the hustle and bustle of today's furious pace of life and what seem to be iron-clad obligations, completely opens the door of possibility to just who you can become. You can then use that eulogy to 'reverse engineer' your life in its realization. Spend some serious, focused time on this task: write it well – it just might be delivered when it's your time.

Don't keep what you learn to yourself – be sure to contact me and tell me what you find! Finally, remember that sometimes discovering your purpose is a matter of being still enough to be present to its existence already in your life – you just need to be quiet enough to 'see it' and understand how it's been leading you your whole life. You can start to thread back all the connecting events, decisions, and people that have put you on the path you're on today. And if that's the case for you now, your opportunity is to look for more ways to *bring* it, actualize your purpose, and put it to work in the world. We need it, now.

Key Points and Exercises

Uniquely You

Ask people who know and care about you, 'What makes me *me*? How do I stand out from others? If I disappeared tomorrow and was replaced with someone just as talented, what would you most miss?' Listen intently to their replies and do not deflect or reduce what is told to you. Write down what each person says. Thank them for 'seeing you' and acknowledging who you are to them. Note any patterns that emerge about what makes you uniquely you and special. Now, stand in *that* space, recognize the power of being authentically you, and let yourself be awash in the appreciation of knowing your own value and standing tall in it.

Discovering Your Purpose

Consider the four access points discussed above to discover your purpose. Write something down for each one: (1) What pain have you been working on healing for yourself for a good, long stretch of time – likely years? (2) What major crucible moments have you navigated through that have helped you become who you are today? (3) What are you hopelessly passionate about? (4) What big, wicked, or hairy problem do you stand for solving or addressing?

Facing Your Mortality

Consider and write down how you would live your life differently if you were to discover you only had three months left to live. Write down what you would do or do differently, who you would be or be differently, and how you would relate to people or relate to them differently. Next, consider why it took you discovering this specific end date to change course (if you did). Finally, what could you do today without the certain end-date prognosis to at least approximate this life within a six-month timeline?

Your Eulogy

You guessed it. Now get to it. Write your eulogy completely and fully from the vantage point that it is delivered by someone who captures who you became in life, what you accomplished, and how you were connected to people. Write it in the spirit that you have realized who you really wanted to become and are proud of the life you lived. Does it address how many careers you helped build or the difference you made in how business was conducted – did you elevate it? Consider this: someone may actually read that eulogy and deliver it for you one day. So write it well.

Half-time

Consider two possibilities: (1) Are you currently experiencing this 'half-time' urgency? If so, how is it presenting itself in your life? Does your new understanding of where this urgency is coming from (half-time) help to give you more intention, direction, and motivation to pursue whatever is important to you? (2) If you are not currently experiencing this 'half-time' phenomenon, look for ways you could access and leverage similar motivation in other parts of your life – for example, perhaps you're at half-time at a certain career level or your level as a leader. How can you direct that half-time urgency and motivation to propel you to finish that career hard and in the manner worthy of your one, precious life in that domain?

Video: *Your Reason for Being that Makes the World Better*

Watch this video at www.alisecortez.com or www.gusto-now.com

Become fully attuned to your feelings and reaction to this message. What feelings does this message evoke in you? What can you do to channel those emotions to add urgency to your path toward purpose?

Part 2

Inspiring an Energized, Fulfilled Workforce to Create the World in Which We All Want to Live and Work

7

Work: From 'Just a Paycheck' to a Fulfilling Part of Life

In the first part of this book, we focused largely on helping you become fit as an inspirational leader. You learned the importance of always cultivating meaning as the ultimate source of motivation and energy for yourself. You learned about how your identity is ever evolving and under your own editorship. Cultivating your own sense of wellbeing is paramount, as you cannot care for others unless you are already well cared for. From that foundation, passion, inspiration, and purpose are available to explore and nurture across your life, and certainly in your work and as a leader. In this second part, we focus on your team members, yourself as an inspirational leader to them, and the tremendous ripple effect you can ignite through becoming a member and driving your business consciously to positively impact the world.

Work will consume easily one-third to 57.5% of your life, as meaning at work researcher and practitioner Danny Gutknecht told me on air.[74] In fact, while attending the second annual Purpose conference[75] in October 2019, I heard the organizer, Aaron Hurst of Imperative, say something along

---

[74] *Working on Purpose* episode 286, Voice America, 7/29/2020.
[75] For more information, see www.purpose2030.com

the lines of, 'It's almost statistically impossible to lead a fulfilling life if work is not fulfilling.'

'Work' means mental and physical activities, paid or not, done in order to achieve a result. If you are a student, then your work is your studies. As a volunteer, your work is your service. Dr Alex Pattakos and Elaine Dundon, well-known self-described 'meaningologists',[76] say that 'our work takes our time and energy, and often dictates where we live, where we travel and how we use our financial resources' and that it is a 'reflection of the presence or absence of meaning in our lives.'

In Chapter 1, we discussed the Japanese word *ikigai*, which connotes having something worth living for. I fundamentally believe that work is a sacred part of life and is absolutely worth living for. In essence, work is the unique gift of yourself that you give to your community over the course of your life. In this chapter, you'll learn the importance of finding a way to make work a fulfilling aspect of life that contributes to you as a person and will discover how doing so is essential to wellbeing and can be an expression of your purpose. You will gain greater insight into how the achievement motive works as a factor in fulfillment and how seeking problems to help solve is an excellent way to be of service through work. Discerning the 'mode of engagement' you and your team members experience is an important developmental aid that enables you to monitor connection to work and how you may want to change that dynamic. You'll be encouraged to reconsider your position on ongoing transformation in your work and the importance of constantly seeking work–life harmony, and you'll start to consider why retirement from work is actually not such a good idea.

---

[76] A. Pattakos and E. Dundon, *Prisoners of Our Thoughts: Viktor Frankl's Principles for Discovering Meaning in Life and Work*, 3rd ed., 2017, p. 167.

Working in Today's Purpose Economy

According to Aaron Hurst, who wrote *The Purpose Economy*,[77] humans have lived through four distinct economies: agrarian, industrial, information, and now purpose. His position is that the instability of the marketplace after the 2008 recession ushered in the need for people to find stability in themselves, rather than employers, and that meaning and purpose became the heart of life and work. He also credits the burgeoning millennial generation with cascading its values of meaning and purpose across the rest of the population to expanding the footprint of these terms in the economy. This meaning movement is now overtaking the previous Gen X and Baby Boomer generations, who divorced their professional lives from personal and civic arenas. Hurst, together with some of the studies he cites, has suggested that people are putting less emphasis on cost, convenience, and function in goods and services consumed, while opting to increase meaning in their lives. These people are having a consumer impact, buying products and services that fulfill that need for meaning.

The purpose economy's application in the workplace is in how employees seek an overall work experience well beyond simple compensation while demanding meaningful work. They are motivated by recognition directed at their unique contribution. The opportunity for each person to express their unique talents and contribution, and be appreciated for doing so, represents the new order. Forward-thinking companies are changing the way they recruit new hires. They are starting with learning what matters to the individual applicant and what they are striving to accomplish through the work. Companies or staffing companies like YScouts[78] then find roles that match that striving. It isn't necessary that the managers provide essential

[77] Hurst, *The Purpose Economy*.
[78] *Working on Purpose* episode 206, Voice America, 2/6/2019.

meaning, but rather that they create an environment that elicits it by helping team members know how their work connects to the larger whole of the organization. That same purpose-matching mechanism is being employed by the best companies that brand their purpose so applicants can opt into it or pursue another more fitting one elsewhere.

Hurst shares what he's learned from Nathaniel Kaloc, co-founder of the Re-Work search firm, and says that in the purpose economy employees want three primary things from their work:

1. legacy – the work they do has some enduring meaning to it
2. mastery – deepening their skills and talents to contribute positively to their identity
3. freedom – being paid what they're worth with an additional emphasis on valuing remote work, flexible hours, and benefits beyond the paycheck.

The freedom motive has been positioned at center stage as a key employee engagement factor during the coronavirus pandemic, as many employers were forced to facilitate remote work during the sheltering-in-place mandate. Workers gained a new appreciation for not having to commute to the office each day while having new latitude to juggle personal and family obligations as kids studied from home. Leaders will be wise to look for ways to maintain the fluidity of home and work life ushered in by the pandemic once restrictions are lifted and life returns to 'normal,' whatever that may be.

Leaders who create workplaces where team members see how their work contributes to something meaningful, or to a larger whole, are best positioned for success in the purpose economy. It takes pushing back on the overwhelming momentum of a work world today that is overflowing with systems, processes, tools, and assumptions that, according to

Marcus Buckingham,[79] are deeply flawed and push directly against a person's ability to express their uniqueness at work. I have followed Marcus' work for at least a decade and was elated to talk with him on air about the book he co-authored with Ashley Goodall called *Nine Lies About Work: A Free Thinking Leader's Guide to the Real World.*[80] The book and my conversation on air with Buckingham serve to illuminate a glaring problem – and the resulting opportunity – presented to leaders, who must realize that organizations have largely evolved to be palaces of control that focus on efficiency and order at the expense of humanity and the celebration of their unique contribution. Buckingham and Goodall maintain that their book is for the 'free-thinking leader,' who they describe as:

> *A leader who embraces a world in which the weird*
> *uniqueness of each individual is seen not as a flaw to be*
> *ground down but as a mess worth engaging with, the raw*
> *material for all healthy, ethical, thriving organizations; a*
> *leader who rejects dogma and instead seeks out evidence;*
> *who values emergent patterns above received wisdom; who*
> *thrills to the power of teams; who puts faith in findings,*
> *not philosophy; and above all, a leader who knows that the*
> *only way to make the world better tomorrow is to have the*
> *courage and wit to face up to how it really is today.*[81]

Please be a free-thinking leader and join us in creating *this* world, in which we all not only want to live but where we will thrive. We need everyone striving for a workplace that celebrates humanness and calls forth our best unique

[79] *Working on Purpose* episode 276, Voice America, 5/20/2020.
[80] M. Buckingham and A. Goodall, *Nine Lies About Work: A Free-Thinking Leaders Guide to the Real World,* 2019.
[81] Buckingham and Goodall, *Nine Lies About Work,* p. 5.

talents and contributions. That is the way we will make work something people *ache* to do, not *have* to do.

What Do You Ache to Achieve?

Recall from Chapter 3 that an essential ingredient in the positivist psychology domain is achievement – that is, what is it that you *do* with yourself during your time on earth. The paths to achievement are infinite, and what achievement means to people can be worlds apart. For some, the prize is achieving a life of comfort, raising well-adjusted children who have made their way in the world, or starting a non-profit foundation – all critically important achievements that can take a lifetime to produce. Other significant achievements realizable over a shorter period of time may include getting promoted to the next-level position, completing a leadership course or starting a family.

Having a goal or something to which to commit yourself gives you a powerful sense of aim and purpose. Being needed or wanted by others is also a highly effective life motivator. People need something to strive for in order to stoke the will to live and remain healthy and strong. Recall from Chapter 3 that a dynamic tension between who you are today and who you are striving to become in the future is essential for wellbeing.

I have never been able to forget the aching conveyed to me by a young man I interviewed for my dissertation research in 2003 as I was investigating how IT managers across the United States experienced the relationship between meaning in their work and their identities. Thomas (his assigned pseudonym) was 30 at the time that we conducted the interview. When we met, I would describe him as an ambitious, dynamic young man determined to make a mark in this world through the work he did. Recognition for his efforts and contribution were important to him, and he traced this back to being the youngest child in a large family, always competing to be heard.

While Thomas worked hard to balance other aspects of life outside of work, like giving quality time to family and hobbies, he ached to find work that would greatly challenge him and provide an important sense of achievement. When we spoke, he told me he was not enjoying his work as an IT manager in a large organization as much as he wanted, but felt somewhat trapped by the constraints of the economy from pursuing other, more meaningful opportunities. He doubted that IT was the right place for him and said he had realized that technology was only a tool to support the business and therefore not the central focus he so greatly prized. He didn't want to be completely defined by his work, but said that 'at the end of the day, the piece of me that wants to achieve like my Dad (who's a very successful doctor) can only be achieved through work.'

Work is where Thomas 'found himself,' having always wondered what his special talents were in a family of extraordinary individuals. Through work, he came to know that he was skilled in creativity, using his gut instincts to make smart business decisions, and leading others. In fact, he told me he ultimately wanted to open and run his own business, providing a service or product he found meaningful, and ideally employing close friends to contribute to and share in the joyful success of the organization. It was critically important to him that he make it 'on his own,' just as his father and other respected mentors had done.

As the interview continued, I was moved by Thomas's sincere, heart-felt passion to know his own life really mattered – that his being on this earth made a difference in important ways that would be realized through his achievements within meaningful work. He was desperate to know that he was 'made of the same stuff' as his father and could achieve on the same level. He conveyed his story with conviction and a rare maturity for his years, which squarely illustrates the importance of the achievement motive in work. I certainly resonate with his desire to achieve meaningful things through work and hope I never lose my own drive to do the same.

Thomas is not an exception. I'm willing to bet 60–75% of your team has a similar hunger to that felt by Thomas. The question is whether you know what their hunger is for. Your role as a leader gives you the opportunity to profoundly and positively (or negatively) impact the lives of every member of your team. Knowing what each person really wants from work – what makes it meaningful and rewarding – is critical. Knowing what *you* want from your work must take place before you can be of service to your team. So what do you ache for? Do you hunger to be remembered as the leader who helped innovate a new future for the company? Who led with complete heart? Who lifted your team members to heights they never imagined they could achieve, like Roland did for me? Be clear about what you ache for as a leader – that's your prize.

What Problem Do You Stand to Help Solve? Being of Service to the World

There is no shortage of problems that need addressing and solving in your business or company, and across the world. Problems – otherwise known as opportunities – are everywhere! What a fantastic way to spend your one, precious life: being of service to help address them and make the world a better place. Be useful to the world, and you'll never be bored or unfulfilled.

As an eternal optimist, I used to grimace at the idea of creating or doing *business in service of solving a problem* – it sounded so negative to me. I thought of the pharmaceutical companies that exist to solve the problem of health disease, the banks that exist to provide loans for people who have the problem of not enough money for their needs, and the restaurants that operate to solve the problem of hunger. I have long since come to the realization that what we often call a problem is equally an *opportunity* to improve or do better in disguise. Now, *that* I could get behind. So, framed through that lens, pharmaceutical companies stand for improving or extending the lives of those who consume their drugs; banks offer the promise of borrowing a sum of money against future earnings to fund a new home or business venture; and restaurants offer the promise of an engaging, delightful experience while filling hungry bellies.

The problem I exist to solve is waking the otherwise 'walking dead,' helping to catalyze life-giving passion, inspiration, and purpose. I do so because I know personally how much more enriching and fulfilling life is with these essential ingredients baked into the dish of life, the difference living with them makes to my own sense of wellbeing and relationships, and the profound difference I make by contributing my talents in the service of addressing this problem. You do yourself an extreme favor when you are clear about what problem or opportunity you are solving or addressing in your work. Quite likely, it will be strongly tied to your purpose. Helping each team member to discover what problem or opportunity uniquely calls their passion and may even elicit their purpose is the mark of profoundly impactful leadership, for which I am asking you to accept the charge.

To give an example of what it looks like to dedicate your life and career to addressing a problem, you have to meet Dr Mark Rosenberg.[82] He chose a life of devotion to combatting disease and violence across the globe as his living legacy. Dr Rosenberg is president and chief executive officer of the Task Force for Global Health in Decatur, Georgia.[83] The Task Force mobilizes partnerships to improve health and wellbeing for people around the world. At the time of the

---

[82] *Working on Purpose* episode 34, Voice America, 9/23/2015.
[83] For more information, see https://taskforce.org

interview, it reached 495 million people in 135 countries with programs focusing on neglected tropical diseases, public health informatics, and field epidemiology. The Task Force is the fourth largest non-profit organization in the country.

Upon first hearing Dr Rosenberg speak at a conference in Atlanta in 2015, I was struck by the extremely impressive career he has built combatting disease and violence across the world and the modest manner in which he spoke. As a meaning in work researcher, I immediately recognized that Dr Rosenberg has been working at a level of achievement and impact for which many people hunger in their lives but often don't quite attain. I wanted to have Dr Rosenberg on my show to gain a glimpse of what was behind this man who had given himself to public service and done so much for the world. Dr Rosenberg shared his passion for public health, celebrated the profound role his mentors have played in his life, and shared the pride and connection he's experienced while serving with his fellow professionals. Dr Rosenberg has dedicated his life to the quest to improve health for the world's most vulnerable people. He sees his work as incredibly fulfilling for himself and important to the world.

You have an unending stream of problems and opportunities to contribute your passion and talents. You may need to employ the curiosity described in Chapter 4 to discover where you most want to contribute. The same goes for your team members, of course. You ought to know what are the problems or opportunities to which they want to contribute their time and talent, alongside what they ache to achieve in their work. After all, the answer may be the same for them and for you. When you effectively unleash your team members to their passion and help them understand where they can make a difference in the world, you open their eyes to their own potential greatness and keep your ripple effect cascading. An impassioned person on the team goes on to positively 'infect' others with the same irresistibility you have when leading from inspiration.

What's Your Mode of Engagement?

Most people give little consideration to their connection to their work. They know if they're happy, frustrated, fulfilled, challenged, or when it's time to look for a new job or do something else. But they don't consider the specific way they experience their work in relation to their sense of self or identity – or how the experience could be different or improved. I've come to understand the profundity of the personal connection to work as it relates to one's overall sense of fulfillment in life, which is partly why I wrote this book. Finding the optimal relationship and connection with work for yourself and those you lead is an imperative.

Somehow in tune with that internal divining rod that was always pulling me to my purpose, I settled on researching how men and women experience meaning in their work and its relationship to their identity for my PhD research conducted in 2003. Later, in 2012–14, I built on those findings and greatly expanded the research to discover 15 modes of engagement. In parallel, my colleague Dr Owen Lynch of Southern Methodist University conducted a grounded theory investigation of the same data, and our respective perspectives provided another level of analysis. The 15 modes were ultimately derived by comparing four quadrants on an x/y axis where the x axis ranged from negative meaning to positive meaning and the y axis ranged from very high positive importance for identity to very high negative detraction on identity.

Listed below are the modes reported from the highest, most fulfilling experience where person and work are inseparable from one another and the work is ascribed as deeply meaningful, to the lowest where work is experienced extremely negatively and negatively informs the person's sense of identity. The most fulfilling mode of engagement (often experienced by priests and rabbis) involves connecting people to a higher power. The next most meaningful mode is 'Living my Purpose,' where person and work are also inseparable and the person ascribes the work to be an expression of fundamental values and/or the mission-driven person they are. Another mode falling under those two highest categories in fulfillment potency is 'Challenging Cognitive Resonance,' which describes people who are governed to engage their intellect and cognitive faculties often while overcoming or working toward confronting a large business or technical challenge.

Much farther down in fulfillment is the mode I see many people exhibiting today: 'Wanting More But Comfortable,' where the person is going through the motions during the day, putting forth the average or little effort, but is little motivated to find other, more exciting or more fulfilling work. I venture to guess that a large percentage of people across the globe experience this mode, which helps explain why 85% of the global workforce according to the Gallup Organization does not want to go to work on Monday morning (or whenever the shift starts) and would rather do something else that day. At the very bottom of the list, in the area where work actually *takes* something from the person in a most negative way, is the mode 'Existential Crisis.' This is a devastating place from which to live and work, and is often all-consuming, very depressing, and quite negatively devastates the person's identity and overall life.

Table 1 shows the 15 modes of engagement, from the most positively engaged with high importance for identity at the top to the most negatively experienced and negative identity connection at the bottom.

Table 1: Modes of Engagement

Mode of engagement	Description
Transcendent Connection	I am called by a force external or sacred to me (usually God or some higher power) to the work I do. This work is 'self-abnegational' in nature, meaning I am serving something or someone beyond my own immediate ego interests. A lot of the meaning I register in the work comes from facilitating connection between the people I serve and a higher power or God, as well as my own strong commitment and connection to this faith.
Living My Purpose	I am doing work that represents my highest values, or I feel the work represents my purpose for living. I catch myself thinking, 'I'm doing the work I'm supposed to be doing.' In many ways, the work I do is a personification of who I am at my most fundamental core and allows me to profoundly and authentically express myself through it. The work I do is essentially inseparable from who I am.
Authentically Impacting Society	I am strongly imprinting my work with who I am and am doing so by deeply expressing my values through my work, whether traditional in nature or attached to my religion or faith. I find deep fulfillment and it is very important to me that I am contributing to a cause larger than myself, that I really make a difference at work, and am having a legacy impact on my community or society at large. I also feel

	very connected to either the people I work with or those I serve. I often really enjoy teaching or speaking as an aspect of the work I do and feel I am good at these activities. I 'want my life to count' and to feel I've done significant work to benefit a broad group of people, and I want to do the work in such a way that I authentically express who I am at a deep level.
Organizational Mission Alignment	While I am certainly expressing myself in my work, I am strongly attracted to, inspired by, and feel a strong identification with the organization or group of people with whom I work. In other words, my values and the mission of the organization are in strong alignment, and my connection to the organization and its people is the principal source of meaning in my work, though I do find many other aspects satisfying and fulfilling too. The mission of this organization inspires me and gives me a purpose for myself that connects me with something much larger (or more important) than myself. I may be a person who highly values collectivism or being part of a group in which I really believe, and thus I highly value belonging to this group for work purposes.
Challenging Cognitive Resonance	I have a strong need for cognition or intellectual work, and the work I do is a principal way to provide that satisfaction and challenge. I am drawn to the particular work I do – perhaps I am even 'addicted' to it – and am doing

	work that feels like a natural fit to my characteristics, skills, and behavioral tendencies. In terms of path, I knew from a young age or early in my career that this was the kind of work that suited me, or I found it later in life and immediately knew it was a perfect fit. Either way, the work feels natural to me and 'hand in glove.' I am dedicated to the work I do or the field I'm in and I find it so innately satisfying that I would even continue doing the work beyond financial need. I tend to 'blur the lines' between work and my personal life because I am 'just me' at work and the work suits innate aspects of myself. I might also believe that I can't imagine doing any other kind of work.
Self-Actualizing	While I am certainly expressing key aspects of myself in my work, I first and foremost recognize it or expect it to be a *vehicle* for my own constant personal growth or self-cultivation to realize my potential and who I can ultimately become. Many aspects of my work are very satisfying to me, and I am quite passionate and energetic about the work I do and the growth I am experiencing because of it. While there are many aspects of life that can help one develop, the work I do is a big arena in which to embark on personal learning and growth, and this personal result is a very central motivation for me. I may even realize there is an active synergy, or interaction, between me and my work, which creates an upward growth spiral to

	which I aspire. I also tend to see my work as 'a journey, not a destination' in that the associated growth is never-ending and never fully complete. I feel like I'm in a constant and active state of 'becoming.'
Genuinely Impacting the Organization	I am strongly imprinting my work with who I am, and often do so by deeply expressing my values – whether traditional in nature or attached to my religion or faith. I derive much of my work meaning by knowing I am strongly impacting the organization for which I work by creating sustainable processes, developing people, implementing a succession plan, or serving my customers. I also feel very connected to either the people I work with or those I serve – whether colleagues, subordinates, or clients/customers. Often, I am a leader or strong individual contributor, and I am focused on the success of the company or organization.
Gainful Resonant Competency	I am doing work that feels natural to me and suits me – my traits or characteristics, skills, behavioral tendencies, and often my perspective or values. I may also even have gravitated to the work at a young age or been early inclined to do it. I take pride in working in my field and being competent or good at the technical or profession-specific details of my work. I enjoy expressing various aspects of my personality or values through the work I do. I also enjoy being successful in my field and earning a good income, as

	those are both important factors for my self-esteem. I do have other things in my life, though, that are as important or sometimes more important to me than the work so the work is not super central to who I am. I enjoy it, though, and feel pride in being skilled in this profession.
Chosen Achievement Path	I may not have known I wanted to do the kind of work I am doing or may have fallen into the work I do, but I find it satisfying and imprint the work with the way I do it. Tangible results and hard work are really important to me, as they demonstrate my contribution and success to myself and to others. The most meaningful aspects of my work are the career advancement, compensation, power, prestige, respect, status, or rank, and feeling of success this work affords me.
Relational Caring	My relationships at work are the most meaningful aspect of the work I do. I pride myself in being exceptional with people and connections, and I feel strongly compelled to care for customers/clients or other people in my work realm. This caring aspect of my work is what really makes my work for me, and it's different to simply relating or enjoying other people – I am actively and lovingly taking care of the people I serve. The trust and dependability that comes with these relationships is also very important to me.

Instrumental Marketable Skill	I am certainly expressing key aspects of myself in my work, and I enjoy and often feel passionate about the work I do. I likely live a very full life or have other things that are also very important to me outside of work, whether they are hobbies, other interests, my family, or my faith. I am happy with the work I've chosen and take pride in being competent and good at the work while achieving strong results. I recognize that I am primarily exchanging skills for an income or work–life harmony that affords me access to other really important parts of my life, or I simply don't expect work to provide more meaning beyond these things ('work is work'). I have many other parts of my life that make me 'me,' and work is only a small part of that mix.
Conflicted Fit	While there are some or even many aspects of the work I enjoy and feel fit with my personality or talents, there are also a large or almost equal number that are just not working for me or don't suit who I am. I enjoy the work much of the time, but I also find myself interested in doing some other, more interesting or suitable work somewhere else, or perhaps work that would allow me to express more of myself. I may feel held back in my career here or not well respected in this work setting. Or maybe I'm interested in doing something altogether different or not even working at all. I feel conflicted about my situation, but I'm not so unhappy that I am contemplating leaving or quitting;

	rather, I find myself rationalizing why I stay or just settling for it for now. It's likely that I'm doing the right (or suitable) work but in the wrong place or environment.
Wanting More but Comfortable	There are some aspects of the work I do that I really enjoy and I certainly express aspects of myself in doing the work. But at the end of the day, week, or month, there are slightly more areas of discontent than contentment. I am primarily staying in this work for the financial compensation I receive, so there is some apathy here. I would love to do some other kind of more interesting or suitable work. I'm not miserable, but I'm not especially happy either. I remain in the work because I'm comfortable with the work arrangement and it's just easier to stay rather than putting much energy into looking for different, potentially better work.
Diminished Esteem	While there are aspects of the work I do that I find satisfying, they are overruled by a sense of distress I feel about the work and myself as a result. I like many aspects of the field or work I do, but I'm also keenly aware that I feel like I've not achieved what I'd like to through my work, that my contributions are not what I would like them to be, and that I'm not who I would like to be as a person through this work. It is an upsetting place to be that has left me longing to find other, more meaningful work where I can be more successful and just be more of who I am.

Existential Crisis or Tribulation	I do enjoy some or even several aspects of my work and often feel I am quite good at them, but I am intensely consumed by the idea that I long for work that allows me to express much more of who I am or to have the overall fulfilled life I want. I often feel I am wasting my potential doing the work I do, which makes me feel very bad about myself and my life. The problem may be that I either don't yet know what I should be doing to fulfill my purpose or potential (i.e. what kind of work) or may feel dependent on the income or situation I am in and so feel trapped with little or no way out. It is very hard to come to work each day and I may resent many aspects of the work or work experience, but right now I feel trapped and unable to leave for a different opportunity. I feel an acute need to do something much more significant with my life through work that I have not yet found or am not currently experiencing. This is a very distressing place to be.

There is so much you as a leader can do to impact your own mode of engagement and that of those you lead, for better or worse. I've helped hundreds of managers and leaders in the programs I facilitate to do so. You have the ability to draw on your own attitude about your work and what it means to you. This ability is uniquely human, and as you learned in Chapter 1, it is one of the three main ways in which people can find meaning (along with what you give of yourself – passion, and what you experience or encounter – inspiration). It is possible to redesign your work to better align with your strengths and values, and thus reposition yourself in relation to the work – a concept Yale researcher Amy Wrzesniewski refers to as 'job crafting'.[84] The key takeaway from considering these modes of engagement is that there isn't a 'best' one, although the seven or nine at the top of the list are more fulfilling and energizing than the six or eight at the bottom. Your team members will want different things from their work as their lives unfold. Staying in meaningful and connected dialogue about what they want in their work as it fits into their overall lives is a key component of being an impactful and inspiring leader who wants to ensure that work is a positive and fulfilling experience.

It's Never Too Late for Transformation

The work you do can help you learn, grow, and literally transform into someone entirely previously unrecognizable to yourself, which is a key reason why I find this domain of life so enthralling. Many people seek work that actively catalyzes their own development to grow into the person they wish to become. That is why so many people cite the need for learning and growth as powerful engagement factors to keep them working in their jobs. In fact, the desire and need for ongoing learning is an area of motivation and meaning that surfaced in my research and manifested in what I call the 'self-actualizing' mode of engagement. People who are experiencing this mode of engagement actively engage themselves with their work and see it as a vehicle to work toward realizing their full potential. I personally experienced much of my earlier career in this self-actualizing mode, determined to discover what I was made of, who I could become, and just what I could do in this world. I was not

---

[84] A. Wrzesniewski and J. Dutton, 'Crafting a job: Revisioning employees as active crafters of their work', *Academy of Management Review*, 26, 179–201.

conscious at the time that I was furiously working to discern my own purpose along this path.

Over the years of working with leaders and teams, I've had the distinct privilege and honor to witness people literally growing before my very eyes, and have been moved to tears countless times in the process. It is profoundly fulfilling that I get to work on such an intimate level with people – to be with them as they work to access their deepest hopes and fears and become present to limiting mindsets and old ways of being that no longer serve them. Being with someone who has a sudden and major 'aha' moment that can never be forgotten is just one of the ways people transform and evolve to higher levels of being and competency. Getting to serve as the catalyst for that transformation is a privilege I always completely cherish.

I know countless people who have changed course in their work lives to pursue an entirely different line of work. One man who comes to mind left a long career in telecom IT to port over what he'd learned in the healthcare field. The move allowed him to make a tremendous contribution to healthcare companies he served over several years, bringing in the technological innovation he helped champion in telecoms to an industry less developed in innovation at the time. Today, he is a senior executive leader in consumer products, playing an even bigger game there. His work has certainly enabled him to realize his potential and soar in his own growth, while lifting up countless careers along the way.

I had the privilege of being on the path of a young woman who also changed course in her career, with a little insight from a workshop she did with me. Working in the accounting department of an insurance services firm, she spent the days combing through spreadsheets. In the Strengths-Based Leadership workshop I was facilitating, I asked her what she loved about her work. With glazed-over eyes, she confessed, 'Really, nothing.' When I learned how she spent her days, I asked her why she lived her life doing work she loathed when there were so many other ways to make a living. She seemed positively perplexed, as it had not occurred to her that she could do work that would engage her strengths in relationship-building. As soon as she got the idea in that workshop that she might be better suited to sales than accounting, she asked her department head for a job change and got it. She's so much happier – she won and so did her employer. How many people do you have working with you who are ill-suited to their roles and don't know it? Think of the life-giving breath you could offer them if you helped them to move into a role that celebrated their strengths and greatness!

The last thing I'd want for you to do is to settle for staying in any work that does not fulfill you because you fear 'it's too late' to start something different. There are just too many stories in the news and among your immediate network of people about those who started their 'next' career in their eighties. A former commercial real estate developer, my beloved former boss and friend Roland, invented the Interlude mobile chair[85] in his early eighties, and is now developing distribution channels for it. It really is never too late to transform yourself into something more. While you're at it, don't forget to give a hand up to the individuals on your team, as Roland did for me.

Being Human in the Technological Age of Artificial Intelligence and Robotics

It would be remiss of me to engage in a conversation about work in these times without touching on the role of artificial intelligence and robotics, and their relationship to how humans contribute to and compete in the workplace. It is inarguable that these technologies are taking away what used to be jobs held by humans, so there is a palpable fear of the

---

[85] For more information, go to www.interludechair.com.

unknown future as more technology is deployed in the world and changes the kinds of jobs people hold.

I see at least two ways in which artificial intelligence and robotics will change the way humans contribute in the workplace – one is the need for constant re-tooling and the other is being intentional about how people connect with each other at work. Starting with the first, people will need to continually learn new skills and ways of working that they did not previously ever consider in order to remain viable in the ever-evolving workplace. In this ongoing process, humans will be 'kicked upstairs' at work. By that, I mean that as humans continue to re-tool and learn, they will likely acquire higher-order skills than they previously held. Thus, working alongside technology means people will be constantly reinventing themselves and co-creating the world of work. The research I've done on meaning in work and identity has taught me that generally the higher the skill level employed, the more meaningful and fulfilling the work.

Yes, artificial intelligence and robotics will continue to disrupt the workplace. But how humans choose to respond to this new set of challenges will vary greatly and require considerable investments of energy and ongoing education and development. Humans will likely find that they are doing less work that is automatable and more than elicits their passion and creativity – a worthy tradeoff in my view. With the gift of attitude, you can ascertain that losing a job to automation affords the previous incumbent the opportunity to employ higher-order skills and thus enjoy more meaning and fulfillment in their work.

Futurist and author Christian Kromme[86] makes the bold claim that a digitized world that embraces technology actually propels people to realize their higher-order consciousness and will make work more fulfilling as a result. I tend to agree that he's right. I am asking that you, as a leader, be on the constant

---

[86] *Working on Purpose* episode 280, Voice America, 6/17/2020.

lookout for how to continually grow yourself and your team in order to remain commercially viable in the workforce and personally fulfilled in your own life. There is no rest – the world is moving too fast, and so is technology. Furthermore, make the budgetary decision to invest in developing humans over the short-term benefit of reducing costs or improving efficiency simply by employing more technology.

The second area I want to address in relation to humans working alongside artificial intelligence and robotics is how companies and leaders will need to continually and mindfully work to create meaningful social interaction and connection. I was first alerted to this perspective and necessity by author Dan Schawbel,[87] who was on my program in 2018 talking about his latest book, *Back to Human: How Great Leaders Create Connection in the Age of Isolation*.[88] In the course of the conversation, Dan helped me understand that in this new age of artificial intelligence and robotics that presses for more productivity and efficiency in the workplace, people across the globe are increasingly feeling more disconnected, isolated, and depressed as a result of what he refers to as an overuse and misuse of technology. Schawbel cites a loneliness epidemic, and says the depression that accompanies it has the same health risk as smoking 15 cigarettes per day. The world of work used to be a place where people enjoyed accomplishment, meaningful relationships, and a purposeful existence. Given the speed at which technology is accelerating across life, we all need to become much more mindful about when and how to appropriately use technology and allow its ongoing development. The forced shut-in of employees to work remotely during the coronavirus pandemic elevated the need for companies and leaders to find new ways to keep the workforce meaningfully connected and collaborating, as the reliance on technology increased to maintain work productivity.

---

[87] *Working on Purpose* episode 202, Voice America, 12/19/2018.

[88] D. Schawbel, *Back to Human: How Great Leaders Create Connection in the Age of Isolation*, 2018.

There are conflicting reports about the overall impact of artificial intelligence on the human workforce. But hard-skill labor will likely be replaced by technology, leaving people to rely on their soft skills to embrace their humanity. Machines are doing the hard skills – humans need to embrace humanity and further refine the soft skills, including creativity, empathy, compassion, and relational skills. Schawbel says we need to consider what differentiates people from robots, then 'double down' on that. Leaders in particular can create and sustain the socially connected workforce that employees crave. The payoff will be a workforce that is more fulfilled, productive, and engaged, and less prone to burnout and turnover.

As I write, the coronavirus pandemic has been present in the world for several months. We have now been able to incorporate Schawbel's suggestions into real-life practice. As shelter-in-place and social distancing mandates have forced employees to work from home, greater use of technology has enabled the continuation of work remotely. Jobs held by humans were replaced by technology, with countless jobs eliminated entirely as the world lurched forward to create a 'new normal.' What we learned was that while technology helped keep us communicating and productive, it did not satisfy the human need for meaningful and personal connection – either one on one or in small groups. You will continue to be challenged as a leader to find ongoing new ways to keep people meaningfully connected in an ever-expansive technologically dividing world.

Forget Work–Life Balance – Go for Work–Life Harmony

I have been working in the employee engagement and management consulting arena long enough to have witnessed a once-upon-a-time focus on 'work–life balance,' which was quickly and wholly abandoned for its laughable improbability. People quickly gave up on chasing this ideal, quite probably because doing so made them feel like a failure and actually yielded more despondency than ushering in wellbeing. Work–life balance was then replaced with 'work–life integration,' which is a more tenable aspiration. This term connotes a necessary commingling of the two worlds of personal and work life, and designates that both have a place in a person's 24-hour day. Yet the newest term I prefer over these is 'work–life harmony,' because it describes a healthy energy exchange and flow.

Work happens within the overall fabric of a person's life, which comprises the sum total of so many overlapping and seemingly competing priorities. Life consists of caring for physical wellbeing, which includes taking time to eat nutritious meals and exercising. Having meaningful social and familial connections and taking the time to nurture them is an important area demanding time and attention. Whether you're raising children, caring for aging parents, or being meaningfully connected in the lives of others, this dimension of life takes abundant time, energy, and focus. Extracurricular activities, which may include playing on the local baseball team, going on vacation, or taking tango dance lessons that add texture and richness to your life, can stoke your passion. They need time and attention too. And what about the community in which you live? Are you volunteering at least occasionally to help sustain or improve things? Time for spiritual inquiry and development is yet another dimension of a full life.

So where does work fit in among these dimensions? Who has time for work, considering this list? That's where harmony comes in. Work offers a beautiful expression of your existence and passions, and the more you can arrange it within the tapestry of the rest of your life so it all flows harmoniously, the more fulfillment and wellbeing you'll enjoy. Each person has it within themselves to work toward work–life harmony and it's quite exhilarating when it happens.

I see companies and leaders creating ill-conceived policies that impose terrible carnage on work–life harmony. As a leader, you can do so much to create an environment and work experience that will contribute to your employees' wellbeing and that flow harmoniously to the rest of their lives. The sheltering-in-place that the coronavirus pandemic ushered in has taught us that much work can be done remotely. Some employees fared quite well with this arrangement and meaningfully reconnected with their families and loved ones with the increased proximity. Other people craved the social interaction available at work or in the office setting. Finding what works best for the individual to bring out their best is tenable – but it does take creativity and accommodation to manage.

Consider a flexible start and end time to allow working parents to drop off and collect children from school – or for other employees to take their exercise or volunteer in the community before they come to work or leave for the day. Companies limit their attractiveness to potential stellar talent and the impassioned contribution by their employees when they insist all employees start at 8.00 am and leave at 5.00 pm, for example. Why not consider a flexible schedule where some start at 8, with another wave at 8.30 or 9? Employees who feel they are valued as individuals and have a life beyond work will go the extra mile to persevere and perform to meet deadlines and deliverables.

Allowing employees time away from the normal work schedule to at least occasionally attend their loved ones' extracurricular events is another simple way to encourage work–life harmony. In today's virtual and remote workplace, employees are happy to make up that time at home in the evening. Consider the extent to which you are asking your employees to choose work at the expense of everything else in their lives, including their relationship with significant others and their contribution to the community. When everyone aspires to greater heights, they are more likely to attain them. Aspire to be the kind of leader people want to give their heart and soul for because you contribute to their overall wellbeing and see them for the magnificent, individually unique creatures they are.

Beware the Hazards of Retirement

Although it's a less common phenomenon than it was when people started a career in the 1980s and before, people are still socially conditioned to achieve 'retirement' from work, so they can really start 'enjoying life.' Yet when you consider what the word 'retirement' actually boils down to, it is 'withdrawal.' Usually, that means withdrawal from the work activities and social arena that the person was once fully engaged in to produce a living.

Unfortunately, as so many people have learned the hard way, it turns out this approach to retiring from social interaction and contribution of talent is not at all conducive to wellbeing or longevity. Withdrawing from the workforce and being a productive member of society often translates to reduced mental function, depression, poor health, and even an early death. While achieving the financial means to sustain an ongoing life is essential, continuing to share your talents and be of service helps you to maintain meaningful connection to others and to continue to learn and grow; it also provides a will to live.

Let me be clear: getting to a point in life where earning an income is no longer a requirement for continuing to sustain yourself is an absolute achievement, and one to be celebrated and revered. Severing the engagement of yourself meaningfully from the world, however, is not a desired or healthy end game. Having something to wake up for speaks to that essential tension discussed in Chapter 3. Humans do not thrive in homeostasis – at least not emotionally, intellectually, or spiritually.

I'm easily 90% confident that both my parents, and certainly my mother, would have lasted longer on earth had they not entirely 'retired from life' and sat and watched the news on television, seldom leaving the house. My mother passed on January 3, 2019 at age 73 with a brilliantly sharp mind. My father followed her 28 days later – largely, I'm convinced, due to a broken, empty heart. It's a beautiful love story, though I am not convinced it had to end the way it did. Yes, my mother had suffered from problems related to chronic obstructive pulmonary disease (COPD) for more than 10 years. Yet had she reached into the community to offer her humor, wit, charm, ideas, and productivity, I dare say she would have been far less focused on her physical discomforts and pain and been able to find joy and meaning in the difference she was making in the lives of her community. That's the vital gift of self-transcendence, and it comes with being of service to others.

Please don't ever stop working – whether you are being paid or volunteering! The world desperately needs your gifts and talents. I promise you'll be the better for it. I don't personally ever plan to 'retire,' even from volunteer or paid work. Why would I? I'm living my purpose. It goes with me everywhere, in every encounter. Why would I shut that off, even when I no longer need to generate income?

I know of countless men and women who are joyfully and productively working well into their seventies and eighties. They bring decades of accumulated experience and a servant heart that wants to continue making a difference. Paul Garrett[89] wryly told me that he had tried and promptly 'failed' at retirement. He'd worked many different jobs over the years, including as a union activist and chapter president, and an administrator of standardized tests, among many diverse occupations. He'd had a long career stint with the Internal Revenue Service as 'one of the good guys,'

---

[89] *Working on Purpose* episode 236, Voice America, 8/14/2019.

helping taxpayers to resolve nightmarish problems and get their refunds and abatements. After retirement, he found himself getting 'antsy,' and his mental health declining, so he returned to the workforce more invigorated and seeking more purpose and more than just a job. He currently assists community college faculty with technology and innovation, and is thriving. Think of all the ways you can continue to be of service to communities when you no longer need to earn an income. Don't stop working and being of service. Be sure to pass on the message and support those who go before you and are transitioning out of the paid workforce – encourage them to continue giving their gifts of passion somewhere. Give a hand up to those who have gone before you and keep the health and wellbeing of your community vibrant and strong, constantly working to ignite the ripple effect we're out to create, together.

Final Thoughts on Work

When you consider the sheer amount of time you'll spend at work over the course of your lives, it would be a shame not to look for ways to optimize the experience. Work in today's purpose economy offers the opportunity for meaningful contribution and a platform to grow into the best version of yourself while helping others to do the same. Work offers a playground to satisfy that which you ache to achieve with your time, talents, and passion. It is well worth expending effort to find and secure work that is meaningful to you, and to every member of your team.

A focal point for optimal work for you is to consider what problem in the world you stand for helping solve. How can you be of service to help address the problem and what outcome would you like to see? The world is chock-full of problems – surely, you can find one on which to focus your talents and passion, and to work in service to address it. Help your team members to do the same, whether inside your current organization or beyond, and you will infuse a vital energy in them that helps them understand that they matter individually. They will never forget how you helped them on that path. Doing so will inform your own legacy.

As work is an integral part of the fabric of life, learning how you experience your work at any one time across your career will enable you to make mindful choices about what work you choose and how you opt to engage yourself with it. Help the individuals on your team to do the same by talking them through their career aspirations, providing mentoring and giving them new assignments or opportunities to learn and grow.

No doubt, along your long life you will have the opportunity – if you're courageous enough to embrace it – to reinvent yourself and transform to another level of being and contribution through your work. You may choose to do this by changing industries, jobs within the company, or in myriad other ways. I can heartily say that many people will be encouraged or forced to transform the relationship and experience of work as it continually bumps up against artificial intelligence and robotics. Work and the workplace will continue to evolve alongside technical innovation, and it will be increasingly important to seek new ways to achieve work–life harmony.

Finally – and the pun is fully intended here – never let retirement become your end game. Having a reason to get up in the morning and know you make a difference goes a long way to stoking the will to live. Remember that the world needs your talents, passion, and contribution for as long as you have breath in your lungs – being of service is a tremendous anti-death serum. Next, you'll see how everything you've learned so far about your own relationship with yourself can assist in your work in helping those you lead become the best versions of themselves through the enriching experiences you create at work.

Key Points and Exercises

Your Mindset

Take stock of your mindset relative to work. Jot down a few key words that immediately come to mind about how you view it. A necessary evil? A way to spend time? A contribution of you as a person? Once you bring to consciousness your mindset on work, you have a starting place to evaluate the extent to which attitude serves you as an employee and leader, and you will be able to start considering where you might have the opportunity to grow and change.

Your Passion

What problem or opportunity summons your passion? Where do you wish to be of service – in your community and in the company for which you work? What problems do the people you lead want to solve? How can you help them to take action?

Modes of Engagement

Read the 15 modes of engagement and consider which you're experiencing today. Reflect on whether there is a different mode you'd prefer to be living and working from. What would it take for you to get there? Consider where you think each member of your team is (remember, you're only speculating on their behalf at this point) and open a conversation with each one to explore in which mode they currently experience their work and whether there is an alternate mode they prefer. What could you each do to make it so?

Transformation

Where in your life, work or leadership do you desire transformation? Why? How can you envision realizing that transformation? Through what process? What aspects covered in this book (like passion, grit, curiosity, ache to achieve, etc.) can you leverage? How can you help your team members transform themselves to a higher level of performance and therefore claim more of their greatness?

Re-tooling

Identify an area in your professional life where you can re-tool 'up' to make yourself more valuable to your company and add bench strength to your career. This may be an investment in emotional intelligence training or strategic planning, as two simple examples. Commit to whatever you identify and see it through for each person on your team as well.

Work–Life Harmony

Create and circulate a poll or survey to your team asking for their input on what they believe would elicit optimal work–life harmony for them. It would be fun to start by asking them how they would define work–life harmony. Perhaps you can give them a list of new procedures or operational ways of working that you might consider offering them (like a flex start/end to the day, or giving them the option to devote 10 per cent of their work week to special projects within your organization that fuel their passions or interests).

The Hazards of Retirement

What would you do with your time to express or cultivate your passions (what you give to the world) when you no longer depend on earning an income? For those on your team who are considering retirement, engage them in conversation about what they plan to do with themselves, their time and energy once they retire. Is there a way to utilize their talents in a different way in the same organization? Or perhaps dial back their time a little while still keeping them around?

Video: *Working in Today's Purpose Economy*

Watch this video at www.alisecortez.com or www.gusto-now.com

Consider three ways to elevate your own experience of work and that of your team members.

8

Purpose-inspired Leadership That Enlivens the Workforce

You have been on a powerful inner journey as you've digested the contents of this book and worked through the accompanying exercises and videos. You now understand you are constantly evolving as a leader and how to manage the language of your story in reflection of your emerging identity. You know how to take care of yourself and your team's wellbeing. You've become a 'moment hunter' and are constantly discovering meaning across your life while helping your teammates do the same. Passion and inspiration are your constant companions as you navigate each day, and you leverage them as meaning agents and powerful sources of energy. You've stepped further into the path of purpose, perhaps even having articulated a powerful purpose statement or *ikigai* expression. And you're now more aware than ever of the opportunities work can present to enrich your team members' lives immensely.

So let's get to some specific areas you'll want to develop for yourself as an inspirational leader who enlivens everyone with whom you work. People are hungry for a sound source of direction and possibility, for a leader who shows them that there really is a way through whatever harsh reality they might be facing or whatever new, uncharted territory that allures them. They want someone who will help them to understand how their individual work contributes to the organization's larger whole and mission. We call those people leaders, and they are desperately needed – especially in the constant flux of rapid technological advance, economic change, and now the aftermath of the coronavirus pandemic.

Over the course of the last half-century, various 'silver bullet' strategies have been identified for effective leadership. Democratic leadership is characterized by enlisting the team to help make decisions alongside the leader. Spearheading change is the hallmark of transformational leadership. Charismatic leaders lead by affecting and orienting followers to their values and beliefs as they model them. Visionary leaders lead by knowing where to go and realizing their vision through people. Servant leaders focus on the growth and wellbeing of the people and communities to which they belong. But at the end of the day, what do all these perspectives have in common that unifies leadership? The answer is that being a leader necessitates having followers.

That begs the question: How do you become someone people *want* to follow? After all, they do have choices. In the purpose economy, you lead by being an effective supplier of meaning and purpose and *inspiring people to their own greatness* – something on which leadership authority Dr Lance Secretan[90] and I agree heartily and that we discussed on air when we focused on his book *The Bellwether Effect: Stop Following, Start Inspiring.*[91] Underlying the philosophy of inspirational leadership is the reality that people are a full reserve of potential who thrive and realize their own greatness when inspired to do so.

An article in *Entrepreneur* magazine[92] described an inspirational leader as working from the following seven characteristics:

---

[90] *Working on Purpose* episode 194, Voice America, 10/24/2018.

[91] L. Secretan, *The Bellwether Effect: Stop Following, Start Inspiring*, 2018.

[92] www.entrepreneur.com/article/252916.

- They express unerring positivity.
- They are grateful to their team.
- They have a crystal-clear vision for the future.
- They listen.
- They communicate impeccably.
- They are trustworthy.
- They are passionate.

In this chapter, these characteristics are interwoven into the discourse about purpose-inspired leadership that enlivens the workforce by igniting passion and elevating cause, in each person and the organization. You'll learn some helpful ways in which new leaders have stepped into their roles and what can inspire that journey for yourself. Becoming someone others can't resist following comes partly from living from your own conviction and letting it shine through your words and deeds. You'll become acquainted with the importance and general approach to creating meaning-enriched and purpose-inspired cultures at work that draw people to them, rather than repel and disengage them. You'll learn how purpose is memorialized through stories you craft about team members' contributions and how the organization is making an impact in the world.

You will also gain a deeper understanding about the importance of a diverse workforce that embraces each individual's uniqueness and how motivation is good for the team. You will learn to lead people to where you see they can grow, not where they stand today. People crave to know that they are valued and appreciated, and you will learn a simple method to effectively communicate your appreciation. Helping to build and elevate the careers of those around you and developing a legacy for your own leadership are discussed as important leadership differentiators. Finally, you will start to consider how the coronavirus's forced hard reboot of work and business has ushered in an opportunity to completely re-evaluate your company or department's workplace practices in order to reinvent them for a future where people want to work.

Stepping Up and into Leadership

Over more than 20 years in the human capital industry, starting in the late 1990s recruiting IT professionals, I have been reminded of countless stories witnessing people step into their first leadership roles. Their reasons were incredibly diverse. A catalyst or unique impetus was usually present to elicit the move, but still it takes stepping into the role of leadership or requesting that it happen.

I've had the privilege of working with thousands of first-time supervisors and managers over the years conducting leadership development sessions and consulting. There is something so incredibly inspiring about watching a person venture into their first role managing others, and the spectrum of responses is vast. Some people are quite cavalier about their departure as individual contributors and spring confidently into the role of supervising the work of others, grossly overestimating their talents. Other new managers take their responsibility quite seriously and worry about whether they are made of the requisite material to handle it. Still others didn't really want the role in the first place and are looking to rid themselves of the job as soon as they can. Then there is the group of people somewhere in the middle, who lean into the opportunity and hang on for the ride.

I've had the opportunity to conduct new supervisor or manager training with a few hundred such new inductees while working with Texas Instruments with such training in English in Dallas and in Spanish in their Mexico operations. Through work coaching new managers how to interpret and improve their employee engagement scores, I had the privilege of serving many pharmaceutical companies, including Johnson & Johnson and Novo Nordisk. I cannot emphasize enough the importance of providing a systematic approach and training for new supervisors or managers to help guide them in their journey from serving as individual contributors to managing, encouraging, supporting, and evaluating the work of those they now supervise. Too often, newly appointed managers are simply thrown into their role and flounder for years, developing bad habits that need correcting later. There are too many tried and true programs available not to harness one of them for your organization – or create a standard offering of your own that embodies your company's values and purpose.

However the leap into the new role of leadership occurs, I heartily recommend celebrating the advance somehow. Let me introduce you to a woman I met from my professional association while I was a participant in the Leadership Texas program in 2014. This program recruits a cohort of women each year and gives them a common platform that both alerts them to the problems in Texas that need their contribution while building a common network among them to strengthen and support them. One day, our group of 95 women had left the hotel and assembled on a bus to tour a few stops in Austin, and I found myself seated next to Dr Shardha Jogee, Professor of Astronomy at the University of Texas at Austin.

As the bus pulled away from the hotel, Shardha and I chatted casually about the day ahead and a few other small polite things I can no longer recall. Suddenly, Shardha exclaimed as if to a few of us seated around her, or perhaps simply to herself in that moment, 'That's it! I'm just going to DO it!' Always up for adventure and fun, and being taken in by the ferocity of her exclamation, I replied, 'Do what? What are we doing? Robbing a bank? Jumping off the bus to go grab ice cream? What??!! I'm in!' Shardha looked at me as if herself a little surprised at the passion that had taken over her and then launched into her story.

She explained that she'd been working at the university for a few years and had purposefully decided not to apply for any leadership roles in her department. She explained she had two young children at home, a full teaching load, and just didn't have the time or energy. But then – and she stopped herself in mid-sentence, seemingly baffled at her own self-imposed limitations – she said, 'No more excuses! I'm putting my name in the hat to become the chair of my department!' I squealed in delight, causing a small sea of startled heads to turn in our direction and inquire through their questioning eyes whether either of us was in any harm. Smiling assuredly back at them, I turned to Shardha, who was seemingly trying to understand for herself just what force had overtaken her.

I asked Shardha what prompted her decision to run for the department chair position. And she gave the best possible reply in service of the Leadership Women program that encourages and enables leaders to emerge, 'I'm so inspired by what some of the women in this group have done with their lives! And I can do more with my own.' That's it, ladies and gentlemen. Association is powerful. So is inspiration. Choose thoughtfully and wisely who you surround yourself with, who you learn from, and who you gain direction from. Shardha was inspired to go for more in life and went on to put her name in that chairmanship hat, and guess what? She got the job. Not only that, she's the first woman to hold the department chair role. Talk about stepping up and asking for what you want!

Had Dr Jogee not taken the leap to step into this role as chair of her department, the world would not now have the gift of her passion and inspiration on such a scale. She is igniting passion and elevating cause, which is a beautiful representation of just what she's doing in service of her one, precious life, as was so artfully rendered in the conversation we had on air.[93] The question for you is: How will you step up and into leadership and further your own

---

[93] *Working on Purpose* episode 80, Voice America, 8/10/2016.

growth and contribution? And just as Roland Haertl did for me at age 19, what will you do to help others step up to realize their potential? You can be that gift to yourself and others when you step up and into leadership, and help others do the same.

The Irresistible Magnet

So much of effective leadership is being someone other people want to follow. It really can be that simple. So how do you become someone others want to follow, give their best for, and persist for you when the going gets tough? By this time, I hope you already know what I'm about to propose. When someone is passionate and working from their own unique purpose, it's difficult to resist their positive energy, contagious enthusiasm, and steadfast confidence and determination in their pursuits. Purpose-inspired leaders naturally attract people into their vibrant pool of energy. They are effervescent, literally radiating possibility for everyone around them. If you're still doubting the potency of how purpose-inspired leaders show up in the world, I challenge you to spend the next two weeks really observing people everywhere you go. When you open yourself up to be mindfully aware of others, you'll be hard-pressed not to find someone grounded in and living their purpose. They will stand out and command your attention. Your job is to expend a little energy to go scouting for them – they're out there. But beware – you may just be 'captured' by them and find yourself enrolled into their cause!

I can't think of a stronger example of an irresistible leader that I've personally met and had the chance to work with than Patrick Bet-David.[94] An immigrant from Iran, he spent two years in a refugee camp in Germany before coming to

---

[94] *Working on Purpose* episode 276, Voice America, 6/10/2020.

the United States as a teen. He entered the US military where he spent two years, and was planning to make a career of it when a friend called him and persuaded him he could make a bigger impact in business. 'I'd never been poured into like that before,' he told me. Not believing college was the place for him, he went on to pursue a career in financial investments and planning and became extremely successful. After a few years in that field and coming to believe he could do much more if unrestrained by the people for whom he worked, he opted to found his own financial services marketing company some 10 years ago, using his and his wife's savings. One evening, he recruited – or more aptly, enticed – six colleagues to join him. The result became PHP Agency, a thriving and vibrant organization of 15,000-plus field insurance agents and a team of 65 home office employees supporting them.

Bet-David is hopelessly irresistible as a leader precisely because he walks his own talk across his entire life. It's his profound certainty that America is THE place to make your life what you want of it, and that each of us have the right to chase our dreams and make them come true, that is at the heart of his irresistibility. People *know* his story – where he came from, how extremely hard he worked to achieve his success. Today, he continues to stand for providing an opportunity for anyone who's willing to work for it. He especially wants the underdogs in America, who others have given up on, to have the same opportunity he had to create a magnificent life for themselves while serving their communities. When Bet-David walks into a room, his whole life and set of accomplishments and determination exude from him. The sheer growth and success of his organization in just 10 years is testament to the power of irresistibility emerging from passion that inspires people to go well beyond anything they could have imagined for themselves.

To become an irresistible magnet like Bet-David, you need a powerful sense of conviction. That can come from a goal you're determined to achieve, a vision you are dedicated to achieving, and your own firm grasp of your purpose. Grounding yourself from any of these guideposts, your opportunity is to stand firm in your conviction and live what you stand for with all you've got. People want to be around others who are 'up to something.' Your ability to enroll them into your vision depends on your own strength of conviction. Your impact is directly related to the extent to which you authentically share your convictions to achieve the vision to which you aspire. Though being irresistible is a great start, you'll need to create a culture that elicits meaning and inspires connection and performance, the subject of the next section.

Meaning-enriched and Purpose-inspired Culture

Fulfillment comes through meaning, which as you may recall from Chapter 1 is the principal motivation of human beings. Meaning can be generated from the work you do and the environment you do it in, and it often comes from allowing yourself to express key values, and to connect with colleagues and customers in enriching exchange. Meaning is also derived by finding alignment between your individual purpose and that of the organization. Think of culture as the organization's purpose (why) manifesting through its mission of producing and providing goods and services (what) en route to its vision (what the world looks like when it achieves its purpose).

I fully align with Dr Alex Pattakos and Elaine Dundon's assertion that leaders and managers do well when they see themselves as 'hosts' at work and create a space for people to search for meaning in their work.[95] By that, they mean to

---

[95] Pattakos and Dundon, *The OPA! Way.*

create a more human-centered, meaning-focused workplace by taking a genuine interest in each team member and understanding what is important to them. Further, being a good host as a leader entails enriching each person and making them feel stronger in each interaction so they have a sense that they belong, matter, and their work is a source of meaning. Together, leaders and their followers are integral co-creators of the culture of the workplace, an empowering position that celebrates the stance that all employees are responsible for creating a meaning-enriched culture. Team members just need an open space of permission and invitation to do so. Your role as a leader is to help people find and connect to the deeper meaning of their work, and then to create the conditions that enable and encourage people to continually experience meaning in their work.

Leaders have the opportunity – and the responsibility if they want their employing companies to remain viable – to create environments that are compelling and elicit daily opportunities to connect meaningfully with colleagues and customers while living their key values and purpose. A big part of your role as a leader is to help each member of your team to know on a visceral level that they are part of something important. Culture in a company can be thought of as a six-point framework, as suggested by Josh Levine in his book *Great Mondays*,[96] with which I fully align and conduct similar culture consulting. The critical components are: purpose, values, behaviors, recognition, rituals, and cues, each discussed next.

Purpose

Leaders are incredibly effective when they manage to make purpose 'drip from the walls' and keep it vibrantly alive for

---

[96] J. Levine, *Great Mondays: How to Design a Company Culture Employees Love*, 2019.

employees. One way Louis Efron[97] illustrates a company threading purpose into its culture in his book, *Purpose Meets Execution*,[98] is by following the lead of Stryker, a successful, profitable, ever-growing medical device company. This organization frequently brings in patients whose lives have been saved or improved by its products for employees to remain present to 'why' they do the work they do. Among other professional observances he has made in this regard, Efron told me how he and his expectant wife learned of how purpose is lived at Scottsdale Healthcare. When on tour ahead of their upcoming delivery, suddenly the sound of a lullaby filled the air from ceiling speakers. In that moment, the tour guide stopped them and inquired, 'Do you hear that? That is the sound of another one of our babies being born.' The healthcare system makes it a cultural practice to play that lullaby to announce a new arrival, and the ritual is that everyone stops and smiles. It is a simple, yet powerful way to constantly presence purpose – why this healthcare company exists – through the miracle of birth.

Values

Operationalizing values is the second component of culture. What does the company stand for and how are those values threaded into the way they do business and treat stakeholders? Driversselect is a company based in Dallas/Fort Worth that proudly claims to be the city's only dealer specializing in one- to four-year-old vehicles. I spoke with two driversselect executives, Austin Kremers and Raumond Mayo,[99] on the *Working on Purpose* program to talk about how they and the team intentionally create and live a company

---

[97] *Working on Purpose* episode 269, Voice America, 4/1/2020.
[98] L. Efron, *Purpose Meets Execution: How Winning Organizations Accelerate Engagement and Drive Profits*, 2017.
[99] *Working on Purpose* episode 138, Voice America, 9/20/2017.

culture governed by the mindset that they're not in the 'car business,' but rather the 'care business.' There is a big difference! Through the lens of that orienting value, driversselect leaders are determined to enact a virtuous cycle in caring for their customers, cascade their culture through their 'tribe' of employees, and enjoy the business results these initiatives have yielded.

Alkami is a digital banking solution company based in Plano, Texas. I spoke with Adrianne Court, its Chief Human Resources Officer,[100] about its well-known and celebrated culture. Prior to airing, she proudly gave me a tour, which started with the group of people greeting visitors from the lobby. Tucked behind that is a vault (as their building is in an old bank building). What's inside that open-door vault on display for all to see? Why, their most prized valuables – logos of all their customers and photos of all their employees. This large visual prize makes the statement about what Alkami finds precious. Adrianne told me prospective new hires have been known to weep when they behold Alkami's vault, moved by the prospect of what it must feel like to be valued and appreciated as an employee.

Behaviors

Culture ideally directs employees to choose behavior in accordance with the company's purpose and values. Adrianne shared Alkami's Essential Culture Compound formula, one of its tenets being the company's value of 'optimistic perseverance,' which encourages employees to stay in pursuit of tasks guided by an anticipated positive outcome. The revered practice of storytelling is an essential behavior in which I recommend leaders develop acuity. Telling stories of how the company's products and services have made a difference to customers and the community is a powerful

---

[100] *Working on Purpose* episode 237, Voice America, 8/21/2019.

way to connect to purpose and values, and can always be done in a way that celebrates the unique contribution of a singular employee or team in making it come to fruition.

Recognition

I'm reminded of the conversation I had with Louis Efron on air about his work with OC Tanner, an employee recognition company that walks its own talk. Efron shared a powerful story of how one of OC Tanner's employees, Sturt, had given notice in order to start his own company. Sturt was given a personal send-off and thank you by the CEO, who recognized his tremendous contribution to the company in front of the team, expressed confidence in Sturt's new venture, *and* extended the offer to return to OC Tanner should Sturt ever like to do so. To put his money where his mouth was in that offer, the CEO placed in Sturt's hand a one-way plane ticket back to OC Tanner's headquarters city. Efron helped us understand that recognition as a cultural operative is not only an incentive to performance but encourages retention and even elicits a return back to employment after departure, which is exactly what happened in Sturt's case, as he returned to OC Tanner.

Rituals

Rituals connote those shared activities that build and strengthen relationships, which are an enormous driver in employee fulfillment. While on my tour at Alkami Technologies, Adrianne Court also showed me the 'cafeteria' at Alkami, which is more like a tribal dining hall. She explained that Alkami provides a healthy and tasty lunch for all its tribe members, so they have the benefit of good sustenance shared among them. Providing the meal is also a way of saying, 'we care about your wellbeing' and is an expression of Alkami's Caring Collaboration culture tenet, an essential way the company and its employees work together through their relationships to produce great results.

Cues

The final framework component in culture is cues, those verbal and behaviorial reminders of the company's idealized future when its vision is realized. Although cues often take the form of a mission statement on the lobby wall of a company, I much prefer and advocate with my clients a visual cue that includes a statement of purpose, mission, and vision. Such cues are often embedded as screen savers on employee computer screens and shown on marque screens throughout the buildings.

In my work consulting with companies to develop meaning-enriched and purpose-inspired cultures, I've had the opportunity to help companies become present and fall in love all over again with their purpose and why the company was started in the first place. This initial approach involves articulating why the company was founded and why anyone in the world should care (purpose), what is it that the company does to distinguish its purpose in the way of products or services (mission), and what the world looks like when the company has executed to its purpose (vision). Articulating these three elements in a way that authentically describes the company and how it intends to operate is the difference between an accidental culture and a thriving, intentional one. Once the leadership team does so, they can then create (ideally with the help of team members) and design operational practices informed by purpose, mission, vision, and company values to uphold and reward employees for living those ideals. Creating a meaning-infused culture takes the commitment and buy-in of all members of the organization to live it, reward it, and vigilantly defend it.

The Art of Story: How Purpose is Memorialized

Yes, I know – you've heard it countless times before, but it really is true: people love and remember stories. Have you ever noticed that the instant someone starts to tell a story, the person or people in their vicinity immediately lean forward to listen in? To be an effective and inspiring leader who lives and works from purpose, I invite you to let yourself be drawn into story. Lean in and listen intently when others tell stories. Ask yourself and consider what makes the story compelling? What do you learn about the person telling the story when they narrate it? Do you learn what matters to them? What they value? Do you feel more connected to this person as a result of the shared narration? How does the story make the point they are trying to emphasize or illustrate?

Anyone can and should develop their storytelling abilities; however, to be an inspirational leader, storytelling is an essential implement in the toolbox. Effective and inspiring leaders are master orators who articulate the purpose and impact the organization has on its stakeholders. Leaders who learn how to thread story into their everyday discourse set themselves apart from peers who rush to a never-ending list of priorities. People need spiritual, emotional, and intellectual nourishing, and stories are a proven and appropriate vehicle. Leaders who learn to incorporate story into how they lead meetings, recognize their people, and speak at events not only create more meaning for themselves that fulfills and energizes them; they also foster an environment that is rich in meaning and connection for their people. That richness cascades far and wide into the rest of connecting lives as the story is likely to be reshared over and over by people who loved hearing it the first time. That's the impact that many leaders crave, and it's all within reach through the power of story.

As someone living and leading from purpose, you are drinking daily from the well of life and can draw on everyday events for awe and inspiration. It is from those fundamental elements that you can weave your own story to help the people you lead see your point more clearly, grasp the importance of your message, be moved to remember you and what you conveyed, and – most importantly – act on it with conviction. People need and seek people and stories that encourage, inspire, and give them hope. Standing in your own purpose, you can do that for so many people you encounter and lead. Give yourself the permission *and time* to tell your stories from where they move *you*.

Celebrating the Diversity of Individual Splendor

Living in awe of the world around you includes taking in and appreciating the myriad diversity abundant in people you encounter and certainly those with whom you work. It's easy to enjoy and appreciate people who share your preferred behaviors, approach to seeing the world, and any common values. The opportunity is to develop an appreciation for people with *different* talents and approaches to life and work than your own. That takes some real looking. You can also develop yourself into something much more when you are open and let different people teach you their vantage points and their ways of being and doing things. This contribution is an incredible gift, and organizations are a perfect international playground to broker this opportunity to their employees.

Recently, I had my third delightful conversation with Dr Arthur Ciaramicoli,[101] this time talking about his

---

[101] *Working on Purpose* episode 268, Voice America, 3/25/2020.

book *The Triumph of Diversity: Rejoice in and Benefit from the Interconnectedness of Humankind.*[102] As would be expected from a man who's spent 35 years helping others to understand and develop empathy and emotional intelligence, these concepts were squarely anchored in the book and our conversation. Dr Ciaramicoli was compelled to write this work as he felt tormented and heartbroken about the developments occurring in society today. His view is that we are living in a time with the highest rate of hate crimes and prejudice across society and in the workforce. He shared that antisemitic hate crimes and harassment had reached a record high at 664 hate crimes in 2018. Anti-Muslim hate crimes had increased 67% in the previous three years. Continuing, he reported a Gallup poll that found that those who hate Jews are 30 times more likely to hate Muslims. So it's an 'us versus them' thing, which indicates a fear of not belonging. Women and LGBT groups are also targeted, according to stats Dr Ciaramicoli gathered from the FBI. Some 40% of women say they are discriminated against in the workplace. At the time of writing, massive Black Lives Matter riots were breaking out across the world in mid-2020 in a situation of simmering racial tension amid the coronavirus pandemic. All these problems point to one thing: an inability to appreciate and embrace diversity.

Underlying an inability to appreciate diversity is often a set of prejudices. Dr Ciaramicoli knows from his long career and practice that being prejudiced prevents one's ability to grow. Prejudice is anchored in being short-sighted and black-and-white thinking – for example, making a judgment about somebody based on their appearance or religious orientation. In his practice, he teaches people to use empathy and look beyond the surface to see what's behind the other person, which at its core is exactly what is meant by

---

[102] A. Ciaramicoli, *The Triumph of Adversity: Rejoice in and Benefit from the Interconnectedness of Humankind,* 2020.

embracing diversity. Dr Ciaramicoli shared his analogy that we all grow up writing a novel about ourselves, and it's based on other people and what they say about us and others. You not only believe what you hear about you, but also what is said about others. If you grow up in a home where people make antisemitic comments or derogatory comments about black people or Muslims, you will likely believe them. 'Our responsibility as adults is to make that novel a non-fiction book,' he says. Dr Ciaramicoli says people have to find out the facts and employ empathy, which he says is fact oriented, slows down the process and lets people really listen to others to find out what the realities are, not the preconceived notions that were taught to them through old conditioning. Prejudice, bias, and discrimination are learned, just as appreciation for diversity, acceptance, and joy in engaging others who seem different are also learned.

People tend to seek their own tribe because they feel safe with people who look and act like them. There's a natural affinity for the culture from which you come, although the opportunity lies in resisting the tendency to block off other cultures. The reason diversity training doesn't work well in the corporate world is because it doesn't last long – it's just a brush stroke. It's more effective to keep convening over time with a group of disparate backgrounds. It is far more effective to learn to value people for their character, and not their ethnicity or religion. Empathy opens the door to commonalities and removes the lens of seeing people as different from themselves from the vantage point of fear. Empathy is the lens to diversity.

You greatly distinguish yourself as a leader – and I argue that this is your responsibility – by modelling embracing diversity yourself and encouraging and teaching your team members to become aware of their own prejudice, bias, and discrimination. It is there, I promise you. Empathy and the acceptance of diversity expand your mind and give you a greater sense of ease in the world, causing a positive brain change that will result in a higher-spirited and more successful company, family, and community, and help to reverse the dangerous trends of bias and prejudice. We can all learn to employ curiosity and wonder when encountering others who seem different from us on the surface. And in doing so, we will be delighted in the wonder of each unique person we encounter while helping to create a connected, peaceful workplace and world.

Imagine a workplace where everyone felt accepted, seen, and celebrated – what a sea change that would be! As a leader, you can help usher in this new world order with the cosmic igniting ripple that starts in your department and skips across your company and back home to the families and communities to which your employees are connected. Never doubt the impact you can have, especially when you step beyond yourself in self-transcendence and reach out to unite your team and beyond.

In May 2020, George Floyd, a black man, was killed at the hands of five white police officers in Minneapolis. I think, exacerbated by the months of sheltering-in-place, unemployment, and centuries of racial unrest, the world erupted in protest. I hope the coronavirus pandemic actually gives pause to the world and makes it sit up and take notice and listen mindfully to what is underneath Mr Floyd's death. Racism and immunity from prosecution will not be tolerated. The 4th Circuit Court of Appeals announced a potent decision on June 9, 2020, that qualified immunity for fear-based use of deadly force was unacceptable and reversed the summary judgment on qualified immunity grounds, which essentially means the five officers involved in the death of Mr Floyd will be held to account. This is an important step in the right direction. Whatever your politics, holding yourself and your team to account on racist attitudes, bias, and discriminatory practices you've yet to examine is vital to creating a workplace where we want to give our best and a world we're proud of and feel safe to call home.

The Gift of Today and Tomorrow

Beyond appreciating diversity and differences, what kind of a difference could you make to each member of your team if you saw them not as who they are today, but who they *could* be – that is, who they could grow into and become, a person that they cannot even see for themselves?

Remember the story I told about my boss Roland who fired me at age 19? He did so because he saw something much more for me than I could ever envision for myself. Before that famous speech of dismissal, it really had never occurred to me that I could go to college and earn a degree, nor that I could see and experience the world by living abroad as I have. Roland opened the world of possibility wide open for me and frankly saved me from living a much smaller and much less fulfilling life. I will never forget the difference he made, *by seeing me as I could be* and acting accordingly by relieving me of duty to pursue becoming that person. I have kept in touch with him ever since, dropping in on him each summer in Portland en route to visiting family and friends. It is my turn now to cheer *him* on as he launches the Interlude traveling chair he just invented. I'm so proud of him I could bust. Wouldn't you like to matter and make a difference for people like Roland has for me? That's impact. That's legacy. And he knows in the very fiber of his being how much he has mattered to me, and how much I love him, because I tell him so.

When you see people for who they *can* become, it's easier to conceive of and award them stretch assignments and opportunities beyond what may appear to be their current capacity because your view of them extends beyond where they are today. Quite often, people rise to the occasion to complete impossible or stretch assignments, in part because they do not want to disappoint you and in part because you inspire them to want more for themselves. In essence, you become the Chief Growth Officer when you see your team members as who they can become and treat them accordingly. One of the most commonly cited motivators from employees is their desire at work to learn and grow. You have tremendous capacity and power to help your team members do so.

The Art and Value of Appreciation: Speaking Your Thanks

There is a simple truth that, when you embrace and begin to celebrate it, will radically alter every interaction you have going forward: Every person wants to know they are special, different, and 'seen.' When you not only 'see' each team member for the remarkable human they are, but also communicate that to them in a way that is meaningful to them, you have forever improved their experience of work and view of themselves. That is a legacy contribution that will endure for a lifetime.

Every day the people with whom you work – team members, leaders, customers or clients, vendors or suppliers – all do something pretty spectacular. No kidding. Did you miss it? Maybe because you expect the basics or worse from everyone? I am amazed how a simple, genuine acknowledgment of someone just knocks them back! I love telling my sound engineer Aaron at Voice America every week what a rock star he is when we record the show. He gets bigger as a human, and so do I. It's almost as if I can feel our molecules dancing closer together across the geographical distance between us. That's more than a win–win – it's kind of *magic*. I am only expressing and acknowledging the obvious – the act itself is critical: it's not even remotely sufficient merely to think it. By the way, did you notice how I referred to Aaron as *my* sound engineer? It's not as though I am the only host with whom he works, but he's *my* sound engineer because he makes me feel completely seen and special. What a gift and treasure he is every week.

In the consulting work I do with organizations and while conducting culture assessment interviews, I often hear people tell me how much it matters to them and motivates them to be acknowledged for what they do well and for their contribution. They tell me that hearing these few words will move them for miles in the future. Yet, all too often, leaders and people within organizations do not express appreciation or acknowledgment for what their team does well. The power of a simple acknowledgment can be amazing. It can mean the world to a person on that day, while a lack of recognition for a job well done or a critical word spoken in front of others can crush them for eternity. Constructive feedback and affirming acknowledgment received over the lifetime of a career can shape professional growth, create meaning and fulfillment, and ultimately ignite greater connection and appreciation throughout your organization, and into the greater community.

In Chapter 1, you learned the three principal ways people create meaning for themselves: through their creations and what they give of themselves (their passions); the stand or attitude they take to any event or experience in life, especially those that they cannot change (attitude or mindset); and the encounters and experiences across their lives (their inspirations). Never underestimate the meaning to which you give your team access when you recognize their value and appreciate their contributions – they are a powerful inspiration. Those interactions lift and inspire them to want to do more for you and the organization, and to hold a higher regard for themselves. I have worked with countless leaders and individual contributors over the years who have confided that they left a role or company because, from their viewpoint, they had gone above and beyond in delivering work they understood to be very important to the organization and were never thanked or acknowledged for their contribution. In many cases, these departing employees had given up precious personal time, and perhaps even missed children's birthday celebrations or family vacations, in order to meet that critical deliverable. Then their boss took the credit 'for the team' or failed to go looking for how each team member contributed to the effort in order to acknowledge them in a meaningful way. In your role as an inspirational leader, learning to constantly recognize and appreciate the contributions of your team members is a distinguishing hallmark of your daily interactions. It's also an extension of living with gratitude, as discussed in Chapter 1.

A general rule of thumb in my book is that you'll know you've delivered the acknowledgment or expression of thanks effectively if the recipient is moved emotionally. Though tears are not a requirement, they are an excellent indication of the quality and import of your expression of thanks – no matter which gender is giving or receiving the message. Remember the age-old adage: people may forget the things you've done, but they'll never forget how you made them feel (good or bad).

Making recognition and appreciation a part of your organization's cultural heartbeat, beyond your own daily contribution, helps to create a place to which people want to belong. You can create this culture by instilling management procedures that include starting your meetings with a few minutes when team members 'brag' or celebrate each other's contributions. Doing so helps to create a positive environment where individuals gain the habit of appreciating each other, which contributes to a collaborative dynamic. Many companies also incorporate a technology platform to give team members across the organization a way to recognize and appreciate colleagues, especially in large, geographically dispersed populations. I had the opportunity to work with a company called Work Proud while collaborating on a series of thought leadership webcasts. The Work Proud platform is one example of how companies utilize a broad platform to encourage employees to recognize and appreciate each other and bake such behavior into the operating culture.[103] No matter what combination of approaches you take as an inspirational leader, make sure your team members know how much you value and appreciate their individual contributions.

Passing the Baton: How Many Careers Will You Help Make?

Looking for ways to work yourself out of a job is a great way to spend your career. You get to grow when your people push you upward in your career, as you pull them up with you. Passing the baton well entails genuine appreciation for the talent of the people in the organization, as you are making a way forward for their future, while succession planning for the organization at the same time. You'll know it's time to usher in the next leader, or set of leaders, when you have met your own purpose in the capacity in which you were working, when you've discovered a new purpose to pursue, or when the person in line to take over for you can expand your own impact. Knowing when you no longer fit in your role or company, as you've served your purpose or things have changed, provides additional opportunities to pass the baton. You enable more of your own human agency when you take on replacing yourself rather than the organization doing so.

It takes a leap of faith to pass the baton on to the next generation of leaders. They will most certainly do the job differently than you did, and that's a big part of what you'll need to learn to gain comfort in. When you look for ways to groom your people upward, you grow their careers and make way for your own upward mobility. I still recall fondly

---

[103] For more information, see https://workproud.com/

a conversation I had with a meaning in work research participant in 2003. He was the Chief Information Officer of a large food processing company. In our interview, he mused how he used to cherish climbing every rung of his own career ladder and then, at some point, instead turned to prizing the *number of careers he had helped make for others*. The navigation of those careers, he reflected, helped the people become who they were. He sat in a quiet, thoughtful moment with me, chewing contentedly on that cherished part of his life.

Once you get to the top, how do you know when it's time to let go? Over the years I've spent in management consulting, I've observed two kinds of professionals: the majority who are reticent to hire people they fear may be more talented or smarter than they are, and the minority who embrace the exact opposite mentality and hire rock stars. The latter group possesses a mindset that great performance happens when talented people come together to create something larger than the sum of their combined parts, *and* that their own growth trajectory as a leader is accelerated when surrounded and supported by such talent. In other words, this minority group of leaders purposely surrounds themselves with people they expect to groom and promote, and know that in the process they too will naturally ascend in their own career.

There are many business leaders I could showcase as examples of passing the baton and pulling others up into leadership positions, but I'm going to choose a pioneer in the Oregon wine industry. At a time when women were rarely decision makers in business or agriculture, Susan Sokol Blosser[104] distinguished herself in both. For over three decades, Susan managed every aspect of Sokol Blosser's winery operation. As the vineyard manager, she drove the tractor, did hand work, and used a forklift to load grapes onto flatbed trucks. As president, she saw Sokol Blosser grow to become one of the largest and most innovative Oregon

---

[104] *Working on Purpose* episode 18, Voice America, 6/3/2015.

wineries, with national and international distribution. Then, at the height of her career, Susan made an extraordinary decision to step away from the work she loved and transition control of the winery to her children.

In our conversation on *Working on Purpose*, we talked about how Susan arrived at that decision, the surprising challenges she faced, the unanticipated journey that ensued, and the good life that followed. In ushering in her children to run the winery, Susan not only opened a whole new world for herself but also gave the new leaders a place from which to launch and grow their own talents to levels they likely couldn't have seen for themselves. Passing the baton of leadership requires a leap of faith, and a healthy dose of courage. The new leaders will make mistakes – ones you've likely already made and learned from – and standing back to let them do so is essential for their own growth and navigation forward.

Legacy: How Will You Memorably Touch Lives?

What do you hope to leave behind after you've left the moment, interaction, company, this life? When you can be clear about what lasting contribution you aim to make to the world, you have a much better chance of it coming to fruition. What will you do with your one, precious life as a leader? What do you stand for? What's your why – how do you matter in the lives of those you touch? And, oh so important to articulate and live by, why does this matter to *you*? When you know the answer to these questions deep in your bones, you can't help but live it – it radiates from you. The way you make people *feel* while living in your purpose is an enormous part of your legacy. Never forget that.

Through my career as a speaker and conducting leadership and employee development programs, I have come to understand that many people deeply desire to leave a legacy that stands to exemplify the contribution of their life. Yet they are so constrained by their fears that they cannot make it so. They fear achieving such a legacy is too big a feat, or simply too grand an aspiration. In our conversations, they often go on as if soothing themselves with 'I have a really good life – I really don't need anything more.' I recognize the tell-tale tone of concession – of having given up on their dreams before ever running after them. I understand. Making a life you're proud of takes abundant courage and often someone to help you battle inevitable self-doubt. Everyone needs encouragement and sometimes just a good prodding to champion them forward – which is, of course, one of the reasons I do the work I do. I exist to help awaken people to their passion and purpose, then inspire them to pursue them mightily to make a contribution worthy of their one, precious life. That contribution is their legacy.

As you might recall from the beginning of this book, I've now written and delivered my first two eulogies – for my parents who passed away 28 days apart in January 2019. Those experiences have been quite profound for me and have done much to shock me out of my own complacent way of walking through my life. Neither life nor happiness is promised to you, but the way you give meaning to everyday moments and what you do with your life and what you leave behind are your responsibility and opportunity. The desire for legacy drives people much more than is commonly understood. As my friend Mark Snyder says, 'Legacy is the translation of who we are in our soul, our deepest selves into what we leave behind.' You will achieve far better results through your legacy when you intentionally set out to craft the desired outcome. Reverse engineer your legacy and then get to living the plan.

Final Thoughts on Purpose-inspired Leadership

Leadership, and purpose-inspired leadership in particular, can manifest anywhere, anytime, by anyone. You lead the charge on your expressed attitude about the upcoming merger with another company, the stance you take in a meeting (especially if your view is not among the popular set), and when you go out of your way to welcome a new person into the department. Make no mistake: when you do step up and formally take a role in leadership, the game changes considerably with that leap. You'll feel a certain vulnerability as you step into that new territory and expose your authenticity. But rest assured, it's the only way to be effective as an inspirational leader. The more true and real you are to yourself, letting it shine through, the greater your irresistibility that draws others to you.

Within the workplace, there is so much you can do to create and operate within a meaning-infused culture where everyday practices remind employees of the significance of their work and why they matter. The practice of regularly bringing in your clients or customers to share how your organization made a difference in their lives is a powerful way to illustrate significance and show employees that they are part of that impact, that they helped make it happen. Your own ability to narrate the stories of how your organization makes this difference in the world is such an important way to memorialize purpose and help employees remember why their work is so important.

Learning to see the unique value and contribution of each of your team members and articulating your genuine appreciation for how it made a difference to the organization is a distinguishing hallmark of a purpose-inspired leader. Everyone wants to feel that they are 'great' in their own way. When you can help them realize more of their greatness and help them navigate their careers upward by passing the baton, you inspire them to passionately unleash more of their talents.

The way you register with people when they think of you and how you make them feel will be a big part of your legacy. What greatly colors that legacy is your ability to recognize, appreciate, and unleash the splendor of the diverse workforce with which you work every day and see each person for the remarkably unique gift they are. Today's world is now ever more interconnected, as we have learned through the coronavirus pandemic. In the next chapter, you will learn how taking all you've learned in this book so far can be ignited through your company's operations to elevate the way its business is done and mindfully serve all multi-stakeholders.

Key Points and Exercises

Stepping Up to Leadership

Where in your life have you been holding yourself back from contributing as a leader? Identify why that is so. What's in your way? Who could you become and what impact could you have if only you were catapulted forward to step into leadership the way Dr Shardha Jogee did? What do you need to help you take the leap? Who can you take on to help step up and into a leadership role?

Sharing Your Passion

Practice sharing with different groups what you are deeply passionate about or something that inspires you deeply. Ask your listeners to tell you what they got from your sharing and how you came across to them. Repeat often. Do it in staff meetings, too, and ask your team to share what inspires them and why. You will learn more about what motivates them than you ever imagined.

Increasing Team Connectivity

Consider and write down at least five things you as a leader can do to point out where culture could be addressed or developed in your company to increase connectivity among the team, elicit more impassioned contribution by each individual, and how the team could be unified in a way that is fulfilling. If you're the team member, take this list to your manager or leader and invite a dialogue to consider how addressing these areas could head your group down the path of purpose-inspired leadership. (Remember, you can always lead from where you are.)

Finding Purpose, Mission and Vision

As an individual leader, take a stab at writing out what you believe is your company's purpose, mission, and vision (using the definitions provided in this chapter) and share them with the person you report to – see whether the two of you are aligned. Very likely you won't be, unless you've gone through a recent exercise among your leadership team to cull this work. If you're not aligned, make a proposal to your leader or leadership team to get this work facilitated among your team. Whether it's us at Dr Alise Cortez and Associates or Gusto Now who help you, or another firm, get some guidance as an outside perspective and facilitator helps ensure all voices are heard and the conversation stays productive.

Creating Stories

Write out the major points of two stories: (1) In two to three pages only, write your personal life story, who you are, and how you came to be this person (this may be very challenging to you and is an exercise I often give program participants as they enter leadership programs). (2) Write your professional/leadership story, including what and – most importantly – why you do what you do. Write out the chief points pertinent to each story, the highs, the lows, the impossible chasms you had to cross and how doing so made you into the person (or team or company) you are today. Find an audience and share both of them.

Sharing Stories

Convene a storytelling platform within your organization to invite employees to share their upbringing, key values, and favorite pastimes with the rest of the team – similar to what Dr Ciaramicoli does, as described in this chapter. You can also encourage them to bring a favorite dish from their upbringing. Notice how the storytelling connects your team and breaks down barriers, inviting new ways of collaborating and solving problems. Be sure to encourage an atmosphere of curiosity and set down rules of engagement anchored in respect.

The Gift of What Could Be

Download the Gift of What Could Be template from www. alisecortez.com or www.gusto-now.com It will guide you to write down all the names of the people on your team. Distinguish what makes each of them different, unique, special. What have you learned about them since working with them? Do you know their hopes, their dreams? Create a vision for each of them regarding where you believe they can grow to. Talk with each member about the vision you have for them. Standing in that vision, lead them every day from it and begin to 'draw' it out of them to live into that vision. Amazing things will happen!

Speaking Your Thanks

Starting today, begin the practice of speaking your appreciation for those in your life. Start with your family, your significant other, friends, children if you have them. Tell them each what you appreciate about them. When you spot them doing something well, even persevering through their studies into the midnight hours, tell them you appreciate the work ethic and that it will serve them well in life. Tell them why you appreciate or value this aspect or contribution of the person. Do the same for each member of your team.

Passing the Baton

Where across your life can you pass the baton? In a community organization to which you belong? Within your own family? At work as a leader? Who can you bring up? When you orchestrate their moving up, what space opens up for you?

Video: *Purpose-Inspired Leadership that Enlivens the Workplace*

Watch this video at www.alisecortez.com or www.gusto-now.com

What are three key actions you could take to apply the learning and elevate your own inspirational leadership growth and contribution?

9

Purpose-led Organizations: The Engines of Capitalism That Elevate the World

In this final chapter, we come to the ultimate unleashing engine – capitalistic business. You've learned how to vitally inspire yourself from the inside out to be fit for effective leadership and live your purpose, fueled by passion and inspiration. Now let's take a closer look at how meaning and purpose can be leveraged from inside purpose-led companies to ignite the contributions of a passionate, inspired workforce to help make the world a better place for everyone. Consider the sheer depth and breadth of resources available through organizations and corporations and you will start to comprehend the force of capitalism as engines to unleash and elevate impact in the world. The question is whether that impact is net positive or net negative.

To situate the premise of this chapter, step back for a moment and consider that you are one person living on a planet with another 7.8 billion people. Those 7.8 billion people have a multitude of needs that require meeting to ensure their ongoing survival and thriving. How we manage to do so as the global population expands is a matter of serious sustainability consideration, further brought to my attention in a recent conversation with David Grayson,[105] co-author (with Chris Coulter and Mark Lee) of *All In: The Future of Business Leadership.*[106] Their book thoughtfully considers how the current 7.8 billion population will grow to nine then to ten billion people by mid-century and how they can live reasonably well with the constraints of one planet. If anything can be discerned by weathering the recent coronavirus pandemic, it has to be that we really are one planet, one people – and the needs of those people are vast.

In consideration of how best to weigh in on how to address this array of global needs through the lens of business, I personally know of no one better than Dr Raj Sisodia,[107] a FW Olin Distinguished Professor of Global Business and Whole Foods Market Research Scholar in Conscious Capitalism at Babson College, and Co-Founder and Co-Chairman of Conscious Capitalism Inc. I became acquainted with Dr Sisodia and his work a few years ago as a member of the Dallas chapter of Conscious Capitalism, which launched an ongoing investigation into how business is continually evolving to serve much greater interests beyond rewards for shareholders and its bottom line. As Sisodia and his co-author Michael Gelb describe in their book, *The Healing Organization,*[108] the vast array of problems we face as a globe can best be addressed in a substantive and holistic way through business. Consider the shocking levels of alcoholism, opioid addiction, obesity, depression,

---

[105] *Working on Purpose* episode 272, Voice America, 4/22/2020.

[106] D. Grayson, C. Coulter and M. Lee, *All In: The Future of Business Leadership*, 2018.

[107] *Working on Purpose* episode 255, Voice America, 3/4/2020.

[108] R. Sisodia and M. Gelb, *The Healing Organization: Awakening the Conscience of Business to Help Save the World*, 2019.

anxiety, gun violence, and racial tension as just a smattering of the major issues we confront across the globe.

When you consider the vast history of humanity, we have come a long way. As Sisodia and Gelb depict in their book, we've evolved from the ages of conquering empires to ministering to the needs of specific people, from conquering the masses through violence and the imposition of slavery to unleashing caring as a way to be in the world and do business. Today, organizations can embrace a healing stance by adopting three principles. First, the authors advocate assuming the moral responsibility to prevent and alleviate unnecessary suffering in the world, which includes never abusing power and minimizing hierarchy. Recognizing that employees are also stakeholders is the second principle; it includes a stance of looking for every opportunity that brings joy, play, and love to work. Finally, their third principle is that organizations define, communicate, and live by a healing purpose. Cleverly, the word 'HEALING' is an acronym for organizations that are: Heroic, Evolving, Actionable, Loving, Inspiring, Natural, and Grounded.

Sisodia and Gelb declare in *The Healing Organization* that once someone understands how capitalism can evolve to meet genuine human needs – creating value, being of service to one another, and fulfilling our own self-interests in a much richer, deeper way – why would you consider doing anything else and settling for less? Indeed, that is the question this chapter invites for your consideration, starting with you at the center as a vibrant, inspirational leader anchored in purpose. In this chapter, you will become further acquainted with the principles of conscious capitalism and the promise they offer to steward a way of doing business that works for all stakeholders. You'll be introduced to new ways to do business in the purpose economy and meet a few enlightened, purpose-led organizations that are leading the way today.

Conscious Capitalism: Mindful Profiteering That Elevates Business

I am heartened by the message in Aaron Hurst's *The Purpose Economy* that business has undeniably been altered since the recession of 2008, when people began to look more toward meaning and purpose. Financially devastated by the downturn in the economy, people chose to move away from the traditional anchors of financial gain and stability. Alongside this, it seems more business people have evolved their mentality to embrace the idea their businesses exist not just to 'make a pile of bank,' or to serve principally the shareholder, but also to make contributions to the respective community and world at large. There is so much work to be done across the world in the service of humanity.

Increasingly, the Conscious Capitalism movement is gaining steam, with about 20 like-minded organizations pushing for change to embrace stakeholder capitalism. The term 'stakeholder capitalism' refers to a market system where companies consider the interests of all their stakeholders, which include employees, suppliers, customers, partners or collaborators, the community and the planet, as well as its principle investors. JUST Capital[109] is a 501(c)3 organization that measures and ranks companies on the issues Americans care about most so consumers can then act on that knowledge. Another example is The Coalition for Inclusive Capitalism, a non-profit and global movement on a mission 'to engage leaders across business, government, and civil sectors and encourage them to practice and invest in ways that extend the opportunities and benefits of our economic system to everyone.'[110] Dedicated as a community for non-profit organizations, IC Promise[111] is another organization that

---

[109] See www.justcapital.com
[110] See www.inc-cap.com
[111] See www.icpromise.com

exists to serve non-profit leaders across the globe to make an impact, create a community, and promise to be there for their members along the way. Such organizations are out to continue the process of reshaping how business is done in order to make a positive contribution across the world.

To distinguish Conscious Capitalism,[112] this membership organization exists to support business leaders across the globe in elevating humanity through business by providing learning-focused meetings and conferences and transformational storytelling to reinforce how capitalism can be a powerful force for good when pursued and practiced conscientiously. Conscious businesses are galvanized by higher purposes that serve, align, and integrate the interests of all their major stakeholders. Business leaders who subscribe to the principles of conscious capitalism follow the credo 'do no harm,' meaning no intrinsic harm to humans or the environment. Further, their businesses operate and report on the triple-bottom-line model of profit, people, and planet, which indicates that their targets extend beyond financial bottom-line results. On its website, Conscious Capitalism (2020) declares:

> *We believe that business is good because it creates value, it is ethical because it is based on voluntary exchange, it is noble because it can elevate our existence, and it is heroic because it lifts people out of poverty and creates prosperity. Free enterprise capitalism is the most powerful system for social cooperation and human progress ever conceived. It is one of the most compelling ideas we humans have ever had. But we can aspire to even more.*

This is a compelling call to action that starts with you. Everything in this book beckons you to reach deeper into yourself, through your leadership across your team, and

---

[112] See www.consciouscapitalism.org

through the way you conduct business in your company to reach for more. More awareness, more effort, more heart, more service.

Imagine the realization of this promise as offered by the Conscious Capitalism organization for conscious business practitioners:

> *Their higher state of consciousness makes visible to them the interdependencies that exist across all stakeholders, allowing them to discover and harvest synergies from situations that otherwise seem replete with trade-offs. They have conscious leaders who are driven by service to the company's purpose, all the people the business touches, and the planet we all share together. Conscious businesses have trusting, authentic, innovative and caring cultures that make working there a source of both personal growth and professional fulfillment. They endeavor to create financial, intellectual, social, cultural, emotional, spiritual, physical and ecological wealth for all their stakeholders.*

The vision of Conscious Capitalism is one I hope inspires you to your core, as a purpose-inspired mission ought to do. Imagine this possibility, and you will spring into each day determined to champion its realization.

Another organization that has given powerful voice to the ideals of conscious capitalism is The Business Roundtable,[113] which is self-described as a non-profit association of chief executive officers of America's leading companies working to promote a thriving US economy and expanded opportunities for all Americans through sound public policy. On August 29, 2019, the organization announced the release of a new Statement of Purpose of a Corporation, which moves away from shareholder primacy and includes commitment to all stakeholders (Business Roundtable 2019). Signed by 181

---

[113] See www.businessroundtable.org.

CEOs who commit to lead their companies for the benefit of all stakeholders – customers, employees, suppliers, communities, and shareholders – it raised quite a debate among dissenters. Arguments have been levied against it, declaring that it is impossible to serve more than one master – the shareholder. Others smirk that once there's a downturn or any kind of economic challenge, these 'enlightened' business leaders will turn right back to their old practices of cutting staff and costs to maintain bottom-line business results to stay in good stead with shareholders. Yet, even in the midst of the COVID-19 pandemic, as companies struggled with reduced revenues, there were many instances of CEOs either taking a substantial pay cut or foregoing salaries altogether in order to retain more employees. The key takeaway is that companies are far more likely to achieve stakeholder capitalism when they actually aim for it.

New Ways to Do Business in the Purpose Economy

Business, and the way it's conducted, continues to evolve in part fueled by the work of the Conscious Capitalism movement and other similar organizations discussed earlier to push beyond shareholder primacy, by aiming to serve all stakeholders and provide access to meaning and purpose in the purpose economy. Additionally, as society increasingly evolves toward a higher consciousness through education and practiced values, an increasing array of new businesses are being launched to express and live the founders' core values. Author and entrepreneur Blake Mycoskie's *Start Something That Matters*[114] illustrates this trend beautifully and 'solefully.' Mycoskie is the founder and 'Chief Shoe Giver' of

---

[114] B. Mycoskie, *Start Something That Matters*, 2012.

TOMS Shoes, which operates on the premise of the 'One for One movement,' and gives away one pair of shoes to a child in need in the world for every pair sold.

In his book, Mycoskie encourages readers to 'love your work, work for what you love, and change the world, all at the same time.' His book tells the story of TOMS Shoes and invites you to consider what matters to you and whether you ought to focus 'on earning a living, pursuing your passions, or devoting yourself to causes that inspire you.' Why choose, he says – take them all. This is what he has done by founding, operating, and growing TOMS. When you consider the questions sprinkled throughout this book, what will you do with your one, precious life, and factor in the sheer amount of time and energy that work endeavors take up, the allure of Mycoskie's invitation is powerful. I like the way he simply describes on his LinkedIn profile what serving as Chief Giving Officer affords him: 'My role takes me around the world to share the "One for One" mission, hand place shoes on children, and meet the most amazing and inspiring people.'[115]

To help understand the difference between the TOMS Shoes business model and traditional ways of doing business, it helps to distinguish the three basic business models used today and how they bring value to customers or clients. First, the traditional for-profit model measures its success based on the capacity to generate profit for its owners. Second is the model of charitable organizations, which recognizes its success by creating positive change in the community or area at large. Third, the social enterprise model most representative of TOMS Shoes – a hybrid – sets out to achieve a balance of profit and positive change or contribution.

Let's distinguish some key terms relative to the social enterprise model that you've likely heard before but may appreciate greater clarity on in relation to doing business

---

[115] See www.linkedin.com/in/blakemycoskie

beyond the traditional model. A public benefit corporation indicates the *legal incorporation type* of a business, B Corp refers to the certification of *business type*, and social enterprise refers to the *business model*, as discussed above. B Corp-certified B corporations are businesses that operate along a set of guidelines designed 'to meet the highest standards of verified social and environmental performance, public transparency, and legal accountability to balance profit and purpose'.[116] The B Corporation website also states that 'B Corps are accelerating a global culture shift to redefine success in business and build a more inclusive and sustainable economy. Join a community of 10,000 companies across 150 industries in over 65 countries who are doing just that.'

I have had the distinct pleasure and inspiration of hosting three guests on the *Working on Purpose* program who have started 'something that matters' to them. While I am not privy to whether all these guests classify their business models as social enterprises, I do know one of them does – Paul Skinner's Pimp My Cause. Let me share what they've created in the spirit of doing business in new ways that might inspire your consideration of starting something new or doing business differently to elevate cause.

Paul Skinner and I were on air[117] talking about his book *Collaborative Advantage*[118] when I learned about his pro bono interests to help charitable organizations with their marketing. Paul quickly discovered that his own individual efforts to support non-profits or causes with pro bono marketing simply did not meet the need. Operating from his signature collaboration mindset, he founded Pimp My Cause[119] as a free platform that unites marketers and causes.

---

[116] See www.bcorporation.net

[117] *Working on Purpose* episode 229, Voice America, 6/26/2019.

[118] P. Skinner, *Collaborative Advantage: How Collaboration Beats Competition as a Strategy for Success*, 2018.

[119] See www.pimpmycause.org

Pimp My Cause, Skinner's cheeky name for this marketing engine, has brought together more than 2500 charities and social enterprises with professional marketers who offer such services as innovation, strategy, graphic design, advertising, web design, and public relations. You could say that in creating this platform, Skinner has managed to duplicate himself some 2500 times, and counting. He is handsomely rewarded by his own fulfillment, learning, and being inspired by the work of all the causes his platform helps.

Eric Welch[120] is a social entrepreneur and the Founder and CEO of MPACT Project. Founded in 2014, MPACT Project[121] is a movement comprised of a community of people who care and can pursue their passion to create change by being everyday heroes, making their impact on their own time and in their own way. After a short but meaningful visit to Africa, Eric shared his experience with others who caught the vision to effectively solve social problems through the power of business and empowerment. MPACT Project was founded to create sustainability in villages around the world by empowering purpose-driven people to grow lives of dignity, meaning, and abundance for themselves and friends across the world. The MPACT Project platform is a place where people can pursue their passion and create change. It's a community of people who care, and an opportunity for everyday heroes to make their impact on their own time and in their own way. MPACT Project empowers people to live more abundantly, generously, and purposefully earning money doing meaningful work.

While Eric Welch caught his inspiration to found the organization through a mission trip to Africa, Jin-Ya Huang[122] got hers through her tender love for her mother, who had recently passed away. In her TEDx Talk in Dallas in October

---

[120] *Working on Purpose* episode 81, Voice America, 8/17/2019.
[121] See www.MPACTproject.com
[122] *Working on Purpose* episode 264, Voice America, 2/20/2020.

2019, I heard her tell the story of the inspiration behind founding Break Bread Break Borders.[123] I sat mesmerized as she stood on stage and calmly, yet warmly, looked at the audience. She immediately enrolled us by sharing what a role model her mother has been to her and then uttered a sentence I hope I never forget: 'We all die two deaths – one when we leave our physical body, and the other when people stop talking about us.' She drew the parallel that the social enterprise she founded, a catering with a cause social enterprise empowering refugee women economically through the storytelling of cooking, food, and culture, is a means to help her continue to talk about her beloved mother while helping refugee women. Her mother's work feeding communities helped inspire it and allows her to carry on a similar mission beyond her mother's lifetime.

I offered these three social enterprise examples to inspire your thinking beyond traditional notions of starting or doing business. Whether you are considering venturing into something new for yourself, or you want to act as an intrapreneur and extend your current employer's business into a social enterprise-like offering, consider how much business can elevate cause in the world.

Enlightened, Purpose-led Organizations

Purpose-led organizations are making headlines today due to their elevated levels of employee engagement, innovation, increased revenues, and record shareholder value. Investors are now looking for companies led from purpose because, as is commonly reported, they are six times more likely to be profitable than those not anchored in purpose.[124] The organization's purpose gives employees a lens through

---

[123] See www.breakbreadbreakborders.com
[124] Mercurio, *The Invisible Leader.*

which to see and thread their own daily activities and how they ultimately matter to help deliver on its mission and serve the customer. Being connected to that purpose, and ideally aligning one's own individual purpose with that of the organization, is a powerful way to provide the meaningful work experience so many people crave.

When employees can individually see that their work is worthwhile and that it makes a difference to a larger collective, they are fulfilled, will persist longer at their tasks beyond obstacles, and contribute greater discretionary effort to their work product. In my own immediate experience, I cannot think of a company that is a better example of being purpose-led than DSM, a global, purpose-led, science-based company active in nutrition, health, and sustainable living.[125] I met DSM's President and General Counsel Hugh Welsh[126] when both of us were panelists at a CPhI Women in Leadership panel. As I got to know him some through the course of preparing for the forum and then convening it, I insisted he become a guest on *Working on Purpose*. In my view, DSM is a living, breathing example of the sheer power of what a purpose-led organization can do. It is also illustrative of the power an enlightened leader has to positively cascade impact across the globe through the leveraged power of an organization of 21,000 employees, as evidenced by this tweet sent by DSM on May 4, 2020:

> *DSM colleagues around the world together with our Co-CEOs bid #farewell Corona style to our former CEO Feike Sijbesma. Under his leadership DSM transformed into a #purpose led, performance driven company. We thank Feike for his leadership and vision.*

---

[125] See www.DSM.com.

[126] *Working on Purpose* episode 190, Voice America, 9/26/2018 and episode 267, Voice America, 3/18/2020.

DSM 'is the largest company you've probably never heard of,' Hugh says. On my *Working on Purpose* program, he shared that DSM channels its purpose and increased employee engagement and revenues, while guiding its strategic investments across the globe. Leading from purpose and driven by performance, this $12 billion revenue food and materials global company literally buzzes with energy and enthusiasm. Not only has being purpose-led yielded the highest employee engagement scores in the industry and highest shareholder value, it governs how DSM makes global investments in such areas as nutritious food programs in partnership with African governments and cleaning up the giant garbage patch in the Pacific Ocean. For DSM, a 116-year old company that has greatly evolved from its start as a coal mining operation, just making money is not enough. Rather, living and operating from purpose is where it's at.

In my view, DSM is an ambassador among role models and stands as a beacon to what companies can evolve into to make the world a better place for everyone. Organizations have tremendous power to impact even more people because of their sheer size and reach. What kind of world would we inhabit if more organizations were purpose-led and operated in the same way as DSM?

It would be a delightful project to compile a list of companies across the world that are purpose-led, but you can always start by reading Raj Sisodia, Jag Sheth, and David Wolfe's book *Firms of Endearment: How World-Class Companies Profit from Passion and Purpose*.[127] The book showcases 28 public companies, 29 US private companies, and 15 non-US companies who they describe as 'firms of endearment,' which are characterized by their focus on making the world a better place or who champion a human-centered company vision with sound management and commitment to all

---

[127] R. Sisodia, J. Sheth and D. Wolfe, *Firms of Endearment: How World-Class Companies Profit from Passion and Purpose*, 2014.

stakeholders, managing to 'endear' themselves to all. To qualify as a 'firm of endearment,' the authors required the company to have a well-articulated and authentically lived purpose (beyond profit maximization), to be purpose-driven and service-minded with a reasonably priced CEO, and to promote a company culture anchored in trust, caring, and authenticity.

Some of the companies listed and described in the book you've likely heard of but perhaps hadn't thought of before as 'firms of endearment.' They include Southwest Airlines, Starbucks, Whole Foods, REI, The Container Store, and Unilever. Others, like BMW, Interstate Batteries, and Chubb, may be more surprising as it seems they are not as frequently touted in the press through this kind of categorization. What unites the overall group is that each is helping to usher in a new world and business order by operating in an enlightened, conscious manner, initially by creating value through aligned stakeholder interests. They also tend to operate with a long-term perspective and favor organic growth over growth through mergers and acquisitions, as just some of the distinguishing hallmarks discussed in the book. The discussion of these 'firms of endearment' is intended to situate possibility for you in your own organization and inspire you to look well beyond the way you currently do business to find ways to elevate your cause in order to have a greater impact across your stakeholder community.

Final Thoughts on Purpose-led Organizations

Considering all the change occurring in the world, why not investigate alternative business models for a new company or a new department inside your existing company? Beyond the for-profit and charity models are social enterprise options that can provide an array of ways to stitch together myriad interests and directives while amplifying your individual and organizational impact in the world.

One thing is certain: a purpose-led organization must rest squarely on a viable business model to execute healthy profits. Employing mindful, conscious business practices predisposes your organization to success while attracting supportive stakeholders who are endeared to the work you're doing to make the world a better place for us all. Especially in the midst of the coronavirus pandemic and the hard reboot it has forced, you have the opportunity to take stock of what is most important in life, work, and business, and craft a future for yourself that you want to live in. Now, more than ever, it will take each of us individually reaching for and working from our purpose, united under inspirational leadership and expressing our passion through the work we do to address the fall-out of the pandemic to redesign the workplace. It will also mean doing so conscientiously to feed the immense power of capitalistic enterprise to solve the world's problems with an impassioned workforce ignited by purpose. Now, that's worth getting up for – and spending your one, precious life achieving.

Key Points and Exercises

Converting to Conscious Capitalism

If you don't currently subscribe to conscious capitalism principles, what was written above that might compel you to do so? From what you know so far of the organization and movement, is there anything that gives you pause? Where else can you go to learn more to round out your understanding and stance?

Acknowledging Purpose

What is the purpose of the organization you lead, work for, or are a part of? Where can you, as an individual contributor, manager, or leader start to articulate and actualize this purpose for yourself and your team members? How could you cascade that initiative across your organization to ignite inspired performance, meaningful connection to the organization, creative innovation, and steadfast commitment to your organization?

Video: *Purpose-led Organizations: Engines of Capitalism that Elevate the World*

Watch this video at www.alisecortez.com or www.gusto-now.com

What do you find inspiring about the message? What three insights in the message were most meaningful to you?

Ignite Purpose: A Challenge and Your Call to Action

There, you did it. You've read this book, navigated through the exercises, listened to podcasts and watched videos, and have been transformed to a higher state of being, ready to ignite your purpose and unleash passion in your team members! Your identity has evolved – who you began this process as is not the same person who has emerged having read the book and completed the work. Remember, your identity is your core purpose and will be a lifelong project to discover, develop, and express.

To be fit for this journey, you will need to constantly cultivate a healthy state of wellbeing to keep you vitally inspired and connected in meaningful ways to those you care about and work with. Keep reaching, keep yearning – that dynamic tension between who you are today and who you are striving to become in the future keeps you healthy and motivated. Don't lose sight of the fact that you only have your one, precious life, not an eternity, to make the difference in the world you so ache to achieve. You'll encounter many times over your friend adversity. Remember, she's just there to keep you striving and looking for new ways to get past obstacles. Looking for ways to discover meaning across your life to stoke your energy is the order of the day. Meaning is everywhere, yet it demands that you seek to discover it and fold it into your being to carry you forward.

One of the ways to create meaning and access its accordant energy supply is to look for ways to give your passions to the world. It is through the service of giving your creations and unique contributions that you help create a world in which we want to live and work. This will result in you garnering even more energy for your pursuits. It will take hustle and grit to persevere. You will also meet your enemy complacency along the way, so learn to recognize him early and put him solidly in place behind your goals. Inspiration, or the encounters and experiences life offers, is another powerful source of energizing meaning. Your job is to ensure you stay open to the possibility and wonder that are ever-present in each moment. Your willingness to open yourself to the full spectrum of your emotions is amply rewarded by your present and meaningful connection with others and being deeply moved unapologetically. Inhabiting more of your full being determines the extent of your own nourishment from the world and the accordant irresistibility force you radiate.

As you discover and express your purpose more deeply, the volcanic eruption inside will be impossible for others to miss, or for you to quell. And why would you want to? You and your purpose beg full expression in the one life you've been granted. Don't forget: your days are numbered. There is no eternity to contribute your passions to the world, so get to it! And no matter what form they take, your passions and those of the people on your team will most certainly have great expression through work. It is well worth your while to make your work an essential and nourishing force in your life. Doing work you love and/or that allows you to stand for solving problems worthy of your one existence is the order of the day. It is never too late to step on a new path that catalyzes and transforms you to a higher level of being. You are much more assured to live an overall fulfilling life when your work registers as meaningful for you as well.

As a more invigorated inspirational leader inside your organization, you are now better equipped to weigh in on decisions and policy to ensure all stakeholders are served within the meaning-infused culture in which your employees thrive. Your ability to help your employees realize their own greatness and contribute their talents more mightily in part rests on the storytelling ability you have cultivated. Your articulation of each person's contributions and enabling them to see they are part of the noble organization you serve both makes a fulfilling contribution to their lives and allow them to express their own purpose. By working so diligently to cultivate your own passion, inspiration, and purpose, you irresistibly enable its expression through your leadership. This is your legacy, your indication that you have fully inhabited and lived your one, precious life to enrich the lives of those with whom you live and work, and elevated the contribution of business to all its stakeholders. Well done!

What if our whole reason for being is to discover our purpose, and persist mightily to bring it into the world, so that doing so contributes to a greater human consciousness and constantly raises humanity? Join the Catch Fire community of people across the world who want to live with more passion and work on purpose at www.alisecortez.com or www.gusto-now.com. Keep us informed of the progress of your journey.